Texas A&M University

NUMBER SIXTY-THREE:

The Centennial Series of the Association
of Former Students, Texas A&M University

Cadet Temple Lea Houston, son of General Sam Houston, attended school in *1876* with the first class of Texas A&M. Courtesy Texas A&M University Archives.

TEXAS A&M UNIVERSITY

A Pictorial History, 1876–1996

Second Edition

HENRY C. DETHLOFF

TEXAS A&M UNIVERSITY
College Station

First edition published in 1975 by Texas A&M University Press

The paper used in this book meets the minimum requirements
of the American National Standard for Permanence
of Paper for Printed Library Materials, Z39.48-1984.
Binding materials have been chosen for durability.

Library of Congress Cataloging-in-Publication Data

Dethloff, Henry C.
    Texas A&M University: a pictorial history, 1876–1996 / by Henry C.
Dethloff. — 2nd ed.
      p.   cm. — (The centennial series of the Association of Former
Students, Texas A&M University ; no. 63)
   ISBN 0-89096-704-0
   1. Texas A&M University—History. 2. Texas A&M University—
Pictorial works. I. Title. II. Series.
LD5309.D48   1996
378.764'242—dc20
                                      96-17320
                                        CIP

Acknowledgments

Twenty years have passed since work began on *A Pictorial History of Texas A&M University, 1876–1976*. I am indebted to many who contributed directly and indirectly to that original effort. They are no less participants in this edition. I would particularly like to thank J. Milton Nance, Richard O. "Buck" Weirus, and Ernest Langford for their contributions and assistance of so long ago, which remain significant and appreciated today.

Special thanks are due to a number of individuals who have contributed their time, thoughts, and support in various and sundry ways. They include Mrs. James Earl Rudder, Fred McClure, Jerry C. Cooper, Frank W. R. Hubert, Frank E. Vandiver, Clinton A. Phillips, Herbert H. Richardson, William H. Mobley, E. Dean Gage, James H. Earle, C. Matthew Gardner, Mrs. Fran Slowey, David Chapman, Mark Hansen, Joel Anderson, and Alan Cannon.

*In time, these halls will become classic, and
the strong men of Texas . . . will, after we have
been gathered to our fathers, meet in these halls
and with grateful hearts . . . chant the praises
of their Alma Mater.*

~

Governor Richard Coke
October 4, 1876

Contents

Photograph by James Lyle. Courtesy Texas A&M University Photographic Services.

President's Remarks

The history of Texas A&M University is a chronicle of the accomplishments of many individuals—students, former students, faculty, and staff.

Governor Richard Coke opened the new little College on October 4, 1876, with these brave words: "Henceforward these halls are dedicated to the cause of liberal, scientific and practical education."

Texas A&M remains true to that calling, and today it ranks among the nation's largest and most esteemed public institutions. This public esteem is a tribute to the people of Texas A&M University—the faculty, the staff, and generations of students. Through the years, each generation of Aggies has embraced the responsibility to ensure that the educational programs and opportunities to develop leadership potential remain a hallmark of Texas A&M University.

—Ray M. Bowen

Foreword

The year of 1976, the centennial year of Texas A&M University, was filled with much pomp and fanfare as Aggies the world-over took introspective looks into the rich heritage left by those who had gone before. Although much of that year was nothing less than a celebration of one hundred years of spirit, tradition, excellence, service, and accomplishment, Aggies also knew that it was vitally important to find ways to build upon that rich heritage if the University was to be positioned and poised for success in the second century.

Although many treatises emerged from that celebration, two were a result of the relentless efforts of a professor, historian, and friend. Dr. Henry C. Dethloff's *A Pictorial History of Texas A&M University, 1876-1976*, the new edition of which follows these words, coupled words with pictures in a fashion that resulted in an oft-referenced encyclopedia of Aggie heritage. At the time of the original edition, I was privileged to be serving as president of the then 28,000-member student body. As I pen these words, Texas A&M University boasts over 43,000 students. That student body president is now in his second year as a member of The Texas A&M University System Board of Regents, the governing body of Texas A&M University, along with six other universities and eight state agencies.

These points are referenced to give a means by which once can quantitatively evaluate how dramatically, even drastically, the University has changed, yet remained very much the same, during the past two decades. Dethloff, in his original work, chronicled in one volume the relevant comparisons, contrasts, and controversies that formed the foundation of this thing we Aggies dearly cherish, love, and protect—the Aggie spirit. In this second edition Dethloff has, once again, captured in words and pictures the changes undergone by the institution during the past twenty years, and Texas A&M has done so without sacrificing or losing sight of its core values. Indeed, it is these core values of tradition, service, and excellence that permeate Dethloff's work and which have held the University in good stead over the past 120 years.

As my friend and former boss, President George Bush, said in his inaugural address in 1989, ". . . I see history as a book with many pages, and each day we fill a page with acts of hopefulness and meaning. The new breeze blows, a page turns, the story unfolds. And so today a chapter begins, a small and stately story of unity, diversity, and generosity—shared and written, together." The history encompassed by these pages is nothing less than a stately story of unity, diversity, and generosity that was shared and written together, by Aggies.

As one who has benefited immensely from the selfless service and sacrifices of Aggies who have gone before, it is my hope that this second edition will accomplish at least three tasks—provide a standard by which all future Aggies will be judged, cause Aggies and those who read this rich history to re-evaluate and reaffirm their commitment to the inherent value of service, and insure that the heritage and traditions of the Aggie spirit will be protected and preserved for generations of Aggies yet unborn.

Fred McClure '76

Texas A&M University

"Some may boast of prowess bold,
Of the school they think so grand.
But there's a spirit can ne'er be told,
It's the spirit of Aggieland …"

Gathright Hall. Watercolor by E. M. Schiwetz.

I.

A Small Cluster of Buildings
near a Raw Frontier Town

Texans, who in the fragile days of the Republic of Texas had dedicated public lands to higher education, shared the great vision and aspirations of Senator Justin S. Morrill, who introduced the bill to establish the land-grant system of public higher education. The dream could not be shaken by bloody Civil War or by bitter Reconstruction. Texans had long looked forward to that day, October 4, 1876, when at the dedicatory ceremonies opening Texas' land-grant college and first public institution of higher learning, Governor Richard Coke told a handful of students: "Grave responsibilities rest upon you. The excellence of the college will be determined by your progress. Let honor be your guiding star . . ."

Few colleges or universities have witnessed so much change in the past hundred years, and fewer still have so well preserved a basic stability, sense of purpose, and association with the past. Growth, and even survival, have not always come easily. Texas A&M has weathered the pain of reconstruction, political turmoil, and economic need. It has withstood the throes of educational change, two world wars, and a crippling depression. It has survived—and matured.

The reconstruction of the forties, the anxieties of the fifties, and the rapid progress of the past two decades have left Texas A&M a more healthy, viable university. It has learned to live with change, without rejecting or sacrificing the past.

When Governor Coke made his dedicatory ad-

dress in 1876, the Agricultural and Mechanical College of Texas had already experienced over a decade of adventures and misadventures. The small cluster of buildings set amid postoak and broad prairie bore little resemblance to the sprawling campus of today. In those early years the area served as an assembly point for drives that took Texas beef to Dodge City. Longhorns and mustangs could still be seen nearby.

It was a wild, unlikely environment for the beginnings of a great institution of higher learning. Horned toads, scorpions, rabbits, and deer vied with wolf packs for running room. One young student came to enroll and was attacked by wolves during the day, in full sight of the main building. Another was jumped by a hungry pack just after dinner.

It was a colorful, if not always comfortable, atmosphere for gaining an education. Bathing facilities were only one of the unobtainable luxuries at A&M. Governor Coke and the A&M Board of Directors would have liked to open the school in the fall of 1875 but were forced to wait another year. There was simply too much to be done. There was no president or faculty, no resident or dining facilities. Merely a vast, unequipped main building in the middle of the prairie, four miles from a raw frontier town called Bryan. And if the site of this new institution of learning was close to primitive, its initial educational efforts were perhaps more primitive still. While the school was authorized to teach the agricultural and mechanical arts, such subjects had rarely if ever been taught any-

Where not too long ago Texas longhorn cattle had milled about before the long drive to market, Old Main and the "new" wooden barracks stood in 1878. This was Texas' first venture into higher public education. Courtesy Texas A&M University Archives.

President Thomas S. Gathright (1876–79) of Mississippi was nominated to the position by Jefferson Davis. Courtesy Texas A&M University Archives.

Governor Richard Coke, considered by many the founder of higher education in Texas, dedicated the State Agricultural and Mechanical College on October 4, 1876. Courtesy Texas A&M University Archives.

where else—and never in Texas. Knowledge about these subjects was, at best, severely limited. A&M's first faculty shared very basic problems with faculties everywhere at that time and necessarily found similar answers: stick to the tenets of a classical education and avoid the unknown.

There was a difference, however, at A&M. A battle was shaping between the classicists and the representatives of the emerging new scientific, technical, vocational school. It was a battle that would rage, smoulder, die, and emerge again and again throughout the coming years. And, in the end, it would shape a new, unique kind of university.

Much was awaiting Texas A&M: painful growth and days of glory, traditions that would become a part of the university and irrevocably influence the lives of the young men who would pass through its doors. All of this, though, was in the future. For now, the budding institution of higher learning awaited its first students. Six of them appeared for registration during the first few days of enrollment. By the end of the first term, the number had grown to forty-eight. And by the end of the year, 106 students had enrolled.

Within a chosen field there was a free choice of courses. There were, however, only six teachers on hand, so that "choice" was somewhat narrowed. Students, after four years, could attain S.A. degrees in scientific agriculture, degrees in civil and mining engineering, or an A.B. in language and literature. New students were introduced to President Thomas S. Gathright and given a 28-page set of *Rules and Regulations* that detailed their academic year.

Each student was required to have "two pairs of shoes, seven shirts, seven collars, one comb, etc." He had to purchase two uniforms and a forage cap, and it was mandatory that long hair, whiskers, and moustaches be shorn.

These new students were not unlike students everywhere, then and now. Professors complained that it was difficult to keep chickens near the campus. The president lost his Thanksgiving turkey in 1887. The *Galveston News* reported the "common talk" that the faculty "drank liquor and played cards." Snowballs were thrown at teachers, outhouses were burned, there were night visits to Bryan, and hazing became an acute problem. In 1893, a former state senator wrote that he "had as soon give his boy a pony, six shooter, bottle of whiskey and deck of cards and start him out to get his education as to send him to the AMC . . ."

Somewhere between the mythical Prussian that might have been molded by the *Rules and Regulations* and

This photograph of the Corps of Cadets assembled in front of Old Main in about 1878 shows the stark desolation of the countryside—a citadel of higher education in a primitive wilderness. Courtesy Texas A&M University Archives.

the depraved outlaw imagined by some critics was the typical A&M student.

Financial and personnel problems plagued the new school. In 1879, serious faculty-administration disputes arose. The students became deeply involved in these affairs and took a definite stand. The Corps of Cadets by this year was already becoming the cohesive, spirited force on campus that has since come to symbolize A&M.

Critics continued to question the College's programs, claiming it did not teach agriculture or anything relating to agriculture—which was perfectly true.

The new president, John G. James, declared he intended to make A&M into a truly agricultural and mechanical college. The advent of his administration

was in a sense yet another false start, but it did provide more building blocks for growth. He made every effort to reorganize the College as a training school for farmers and mechanics and to deemphasize the military-training aspects of the school.

During the three years of his administration the general situation at the College appeared to worsen. There were still no bathing facilities on campus. The hospital was totally inadequate, and there were deaths from pneumonia and measles. Difficulties between the University of Texas and the Agricultural and Mechanical College over the distribution of funds reached a boiling point in the newspapers and in the legislature. Despite these problems, there was progress in the making for both institutions.

Facilities improved. The faculty was enlarged, and

President John G. James (*1880-83*) vowed to make A&M into a truly agricultural and mechanical college. Courtesy Texas A&M University Archives.

more classes became available to more students. A frame building for carpentry and woodworking stood behind Old Main. There was a blacksmith shop and a boiler house. "The Line" was composed of five brick houses for the faculty. A depot building faced Old Main, and the railroad began making regular stops at College Station.

The fall session of 1884 saw 133 students enrolled. They were organized into a battalion of three companies: A, B, and C. To a great extent, student life was shaped by the Corps of Cadets. Corps life could be very rewarding. It could, at times, also be arduous. New students in the 1880s were termed "fish," a status distinctly inferior in stature to upperclassmen.

Traditions were in the making, but few existed as they do today. Even the term "Aggies" was not applied to A&M students until after World War I. They were called Cadets, A&MC students, and, after the turn of the century, Farmers. "Aggie" was officially adopted as the student-body nickname only in 1950, when the yearbook was changed from *The Longhorn* to *Aggieland*.

A strong sense of loyalty was already developing. An Association of Ex Students convened in 1880.

The first A&M band (*1894*) proudly lined up behind their drum major, California Morse. Front row, left to right: John K. Woods, T. B. Duggan, Adolph W. Amthor, Percy B. Bittle; middle row: Arthur N. Jenkins, H. D'Echaux, William Bretschneider, W. C. Carothers; rear: S. Kohn, W. N. Mathis, H. L. Williams, O. Gersteman. Joe Holick, not pictured, organized the band and was its first bandmaster. Courtesy Texas A&M University Archives.

The first student body of the new college, *1876*. Courtesy Texas A&M University Archives.

"Through his own personal example and prestige, Sul Ross became the father of Aggie tradition."

General Lawrence Sullivan Ross, pictured here in *1863* in the uniform of a Confederate brigadier general, came to A&M with a heroic record as an Indian fighter and cavalry officer. Courtesy Texas A&M University Archives.

A musical group of cadets poised to play. Courtesy Texas A&M University Archives.

The first Texas A&M football team, 1894. Standing, left to right: California ("Callie") Morse, Arthur P. Watts, Atwood Bittle, Bill Matthews, F. N. Houston, Harry Martin: seated, middle row: John Burney, _____ Altorf, Alfred W. ("Mike") Bloor, Milton Sims; front: Dick Peden, W. G. Massenberg, Hiram F. Coulter, Fort O. Ellis. Courtesy Texas A&M University Archives.

Governor and Mrs. Lawrence Sullivan Ross with the Ross Volunteers in front of Old Main in 1895. Courtesy Texas A&M University Archives.

Company and class rivalry was strong, and this rivalry formed the foundation of the Aggie spirit and tradition of later days. As yet, though, there were no bonfires, yell practices, or even intramural or intercollegiate athletics. No senior boots or Ross Volunteers. There were, however, Keg-Rollings, where students would haul a keg of beer from Bryan and hide it in the woods for a secret, prohibited beer bust. Visits to Bryan required special permission from the president, as that town had "fourteen or fifteen saloons, an average of two per block, and incidental gunplay."

Whatever student life was, and whatever Aggie traditions came to be, was molded by the Corps of Cadets. While other colleges and universities were developing social clubs and fraternities, none of these were encouraged at A&M. The Corps of Cadets instead became a single fraternity which encompassed all students at the College. Indeed, the Corps contributed singularly to making Texas A&M University a truly unique institution of higher learning. From the earliest days of the institution, it created a highly organized, responsive, cohesive, and generally well-led student body. This in itself marked a distinctive quality in A&M's development, because most student bodies have been, and are, disorganized and usually unresponsive groups. By the 1880s, the Corps developed a respectability and stability that reflected the improved status of the College. Public regard for A&M improved measurably throughout the decade.

Moderate elements began to press for cooperation rather than conflict between the University of Texas and the Agricultural and Mechanical College. Elements of discord remained, but the first real attempts at coexistence were being made. Governor John Ireland was succeeded in office by one of the most colorful governors in Texas history, a man destined to play a decisive role in the future of A&M. Lawrence Sullivan Ross came to the school after a career as Indian fighter, brigadier general in the Confederate Army, planter, state senator, and governor.

The selection of Ross as president marked a great step forward for A&M. It signalled the fact, as nothing else could, that A&M had become an important and respected institution. He brought to the College things that no other person could possibly bring. It came to be said that people sent their sons to Sul Ross, not to the College. With the coming of Ross, A&M entered a new age.

Even before Ross, the College had begun to live up to its commitment to "teach such branches of

Upon completing his administration as governor of Texas in *1891*, Ross came to A&M and served as president until his death in *1898*. Courtesy Texas A&M University Archives.

learning as are related to agriculture and the mechanical arts," but not to the exclusion of the liberal arts. Between 1888 and 1890, under "Chairman of the Faculty" Lewis L. McInnis's direction, the first graduate programs leading to M.S. degrees in either agriculture or engineering were initiated. The Scott Guards, later named the Ross Volunteers, were organized. A chaplain was installed, and morning chapel exercises became compulsory for all students. The organization of the Texas Agricultural Experiment Station gave a boost to the entire academic program of the College.

Sul Ross not only held the public's confidence but proved to be a very able and effective administrator. The cadets took great pride in having Ross as their president. He was their leader, their inspiration, and their hero. He subsequently—and deservedly—became an integral part of Aggie tradition.

The first issue of the *Battalion* appeared in 1893 as organized sports came to the campus. A&M beat Navasota 9–0 in baseball. The *College Journal* of February, 1893, announced that A&M now "boasts a crack football team." The first game on record shows

Early cadets line up for a formal portrait. Courtesy Texas A&M University Archives.

C. C. Bailey of Salado, Texas, 2nd lieutenant, Company B, class of *1891–92,* in the uniform worn by cadets during the early nineties. Courtesy Texas A&M University Archives.

A&M defeated Ball High School in Galveston, 14–6.

For those wishing to engage in social activities there was a "Fat Man's Club" and a "Bowlegged Man's Club." There were visits to the circus and fair days in Dallas. A social high point in the cadets' year during the nineties came on San Jacinto Day. It was and is still a very special day for A&M. Aggies around the world stage their annual "Musters" on the anniversary of the Texas victory over Santa Anna.

Ross was proud of his boys, and justifiably so. Graduates were employed as surveyors and engineers, as architects, physicians, and lawyers. They became teachers, administrators, and military men.

The Agricultural Experiment Station prospered during Ross's presidency. There was a new mess hall. Ross Hall was constructed, and there were improvements in water supplies and bathing facilities. By his emphasis on the Corps of Cadets, military training, esprit de corps, and his own personal example and prestige, Ross became the father of the modern Aggie tradition. He made A&M a more attractive place in which to live, study, and work. When he died in 1898,

at the age of sixty, he left behind a college and a state that had been immeasurably altered by his life.

Cadets actively participated in the Spanish-American War. Of the eighty-nine serving in the army, sixty-three were officers or NCOs.

In two short decades, A&M made tremendous strides in becoming what it was meant to become, a reputable and established college for teaching the "branches of learning as are related to agriculture and the mechanical arts . . . in order to promote the liberal and practical education of the industrial classes in their several pursuits and professions of life."

Certainly, the A&M student of the first decade of the twentieth century had fewer customs and traditions than the cadet of the twenties, thirties, or forties. There were no bonfires or yell practices. School spirit was still in its infancy. Football and organized athletics were just beginning.

BUT THERE WAS A BEGINNING.

Members of the first A&M track team, *1898*. Courtesy Texas A&M University Archives.

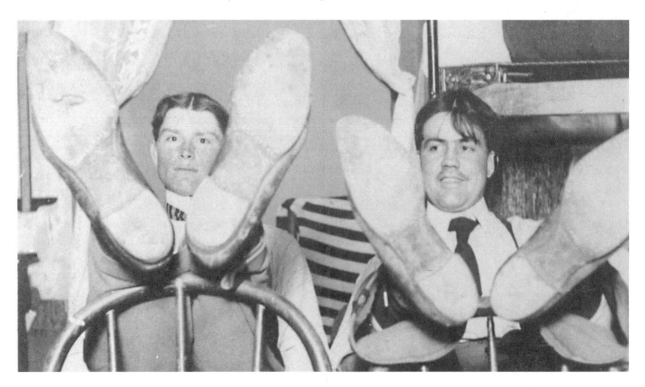

Cadet antics have always been an A&M tradition. Courtesy Texas A&M University Archives.

Professor Louis L. McInnis served as secretary to the board of directors from *1881* until his selection as chairman of the faculty in *1887*. Courtesy Texas A&M University Archives.

Bernard Sbisa, an Austrian-born, New Orleans chef, established a tradition for good food through his five decades of service as steward between *1878* and *1928*. Courtesy Texas A&M University Archives.

Gathright, or Steward's Hall, the second building completed on campus in *1876*, served as a mess hall, dormitory, and for a time as the president's home. Courtesy Texas A&M University Archives.

The *Assembly Hall*, erected in *1889* and razed in *1929*, served through the years as auditorium, chapel, and finally as an armory. Courtesy Texas A&M University Archives.

The A&MC orchestra, *1895–96*. Courtesy Texas A&M University Archives.

The "sink" provided the first "modern" toilet facilities on campus in the *1880s* and *1890s*. Courtesy Texas A&M University Archives.

State Senator George Pfeuffer, the "Bull of New Braunfels," championed the cause of agricultural and mechanical training. Courtesy Texas A&M University Archives.

The Corps of Cadets, organized into Companies A, B, C, and D in *1894*. Courtesy Texas A&M University Archives.

The band in *1902*. Courtesy Texas A&M University Archives.

Hal Moseley, member of the *1900* Texas Aggies football team. Courtesy *Texas A&M University Archives.*

James Allen Whyte, a fullback in *1911*, gives William L. Logan a new view of campus. Courtesy *Texas A&M University Archives.*

The mechanical engineering shop was erected in 1884. Courses in mechanics, including practical training in woodworking, drawing, and surveying, were taught in the early years—but no engineering courses. Courtesy Texas A&M University Archives.

Plenty of water seemed to be the theme of the Corps of Cadets' annual hike to the Brazos in 1912. Courtesy Texas A&M University Archives.

"Uncle Dan" met the boys at the train and hauled their luggage to campus. Courtesy Texas A&M University Archives.

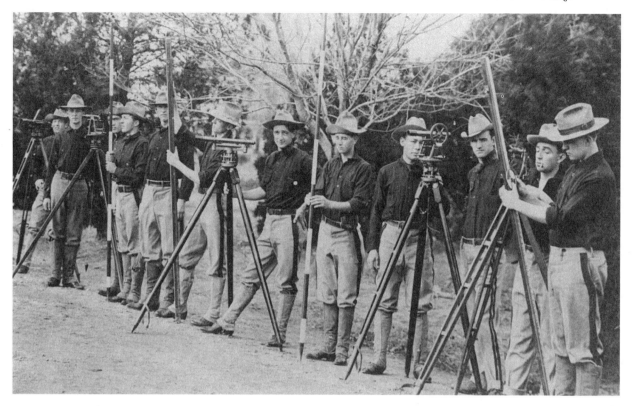

An early group of cadet surveyors. Courtesy Texas A&M University Archives.

The A&M West Gate at the turn of the century symbolizes the proud Aggie heritage. Courtesy Texas A&M University Archives.

Farmer Jim Ferguson said, "There is a real danger of somebody going hog wild about higher education . . ."

Mud was one the many hazards of the annual spring hike.
Courtesy Texas A&M University Archives.

ayette Lumpkin Foster, president, *1898–1901*. Courtesy Texas A&M iversity Archives.

David Franklin Houston, who became Woodrow Wilson's secretary of agriculture, was president between *1902* and *1905*. Courtesy Texas A&M University Archives.

The *1908* annual hike to the Brazos included hilltop maneuvers. Courtesy Texas A&M University Archives.

II.

Farmers and Engineers

In the short space of fifteen years, from the time that Father Time switched out the lights on the nineteenth century to the time that the Kaiser's armies switched out the lights on Europe, the little college in the Brazos country grew flesh on its bones. It readied itself for the time when the country needed its soldiers so desperately on the battlefields and for the time when the nation so needed agriculturists and engineers in the building of peace and a greater prosperity. These were not easy years at Texas A&M. There were student strikes, fires, floods, hazing, administrative changes, politics, controversy, and growing pains. Each took its toll, but each experience added to the strength and purposefulness of the College. Students, faculty, and administrators learned again the continuing lesson that it is no easy task to attend, teach, or run a yearling college in a young and growing state.

In the summer before the new century, construction began on an agricultural building, several faculty homes, and a new dormitory. The directors of the College heralded the modern age by prohibiting the use of any lights other than electric on campus. The 1899–1900 school year began with the usual two days for entrance exams. Again, A&M was forced to turn students away for lack of accommodations. Enrollment for the year reached 443.

Nature was on a rampage in Texas. Heavy floods caused extensive damage along the Brazos. A terrible

hurricane devastated Galveston in
raised $163 for the aid of storm vict

The question of women attend
ready brewing in the minds of earl
Hutson, daughter of Professor Ch
tended the 1893–94 session. Her twin
engineering studies between 1899 a
ceived no grades or degrees, howev
sidered "courtesy students" as a fav

Lafayette Foster served as a con
sive A&M president from 1898 until
He was succeeded by David Houston
ulty of the University of Texas. In late
became a United States secretary o
was a qualified academic leader and
ministrator. His brief tenure as pre
period of sustained growth at A&M.

Thanks in part to Houston's effor
line interurban began operating bet
College Station. It was replaced by a
in 1915, which operated until the re
mobile swept it aside.

These early years at A&M also sav
of a rule against smoking and the c
new athletic field for students. The Si
Day was held in 1904 and was mana
of the Department of Horticulture, E

Texas A&M's "salad years," which

The Shirley Hotel opened in *1906* and helped solve civilian housing problems for several decades. Courtesy Texas A&M University Archives.

Sophie and Mary Hutson, daughters of history professor Charles W. Hutson, attended classes as "unofficial" students between *1899* and *1903*. Courtesy Texas A&M University Archives.

Between *1906* and *1918* "tent city" housed the overflow of students. Courtesy Texas A&M University Archives.

Henry Hill Harrington served as president between *1905* and *1908*.
Courtesy Texas A&M University Archives.

The "Anti-Harry" sign on the smokestack symbolizes the Great Strike of
1908. Courtesy Texas A&M University Archives.

inauguration of Lawrence Sullivan Ross, lasted through the administrations of Foster and Houston. The achievements of the three presidents cannot be over-estimated.

Henry Hill Harrington became president in 1905. His tenure unfortunately marked a time of turmoil, trouble, and misunderstanding, which finally ended in his resignation in 1908. The real causes of the conflict between Harrington and the student body are difficult to pin down. There appear to have been both real and imagined grievances on both sides of the controversy, which finally grew into a student strike in February, 1908. Students, faculty members, directors, parents, and the alumni all became involved. There were accusations and counteraccusations, and a general investigation was conducted. When President Harrington resigned near the end of the year, it was still hard to say exactly what had happened, and why. Students felt Harrington was overly strict and that he had infringed upon their rights. Harrington felt the president of a college had an obligation to fill the needs of his students as he saw them. The answer, it seems now, lay somewhere in between, but it was

hard to find such an objective viewpoint on the campus in 1908.

In the early 1900s, living conditions on campus were quite primitive. From 1906 until the outbreak of World War I, many students still lived in tents, though new dormitories were being built as quickly as economics permitted. There was also a scarcity of housing for the faculty. A&M teachers banded together in 1906 to relieve the situation and built The Shirley, a two-story frame building. It had a large lobby, a dining room and kitchen, and guest rooms upstairs. The Shirley provided temporary quarters for new faculty members while residences were being constructed.

The campus presented a far different picture than it does today. Trees were scarce. A few cedars appeared in clumps here and there and on each side of the road leading to the railroad station. Streets were either dusty or muddy, depending upon the season. Sidewalks, except for cinder and gravel walkways, were nonexistent.

Goodwin Hall was opened for students in 1908. Faculty rank and salary were "modernized" in 1909. Assistants received $800 for twelve months, instruc-

The Ross Volunteers in 1901. Courtesy Texas A&M University Archives.

tors began at $1,000 a year, and full professors' salaries ranged from $1,800 to $2,700 annually.

In 1909, enrollment stood at 757. As the minutes of the board of directors stated, "107 more than there are accommodations for" and "more coming on every train." In June of 1910, the directors authorized the A&M College Club to build the "Shirley Annex." Plans were prepared for two new dormitories, Milner and Leggett halls. An engineering building was completed in 1909. Fire destroyed the Mess Hall in 1911, but a temporary, tin-roofed dining hall and kitchen were erected that same day, and meals continued without interruption.

Disaster struck again in 1912, when Old Main, containing most of the records of the College, was totally destroyed by fire.

In recognition of the growth and new importance of the agricultural curriculum, the board created the School of Agriculture in 1911 and named Edwin J. Kyle as its first dean. Kyle played a major role in initiating correspondence courses for farmers and students and in organizing and directing the Farmers' Short Courses. Both programs marked the advent of organized extension services on the campus. Kyle was also active in support of the A&M sports program, and Kyle Field was later named in his honor.

Problems and negotiations continued with the University of Texas over the allocation of funds. A joint meeting in 1909 provided a general agreement that the institutions should be formally separated, administratively and financially. However, in 1911, a constitutional amendment asking for separation failed to pass the House, and the problem remained as unresolved as ever.

Officials from both schools met again in 1913 and once more resolved to settle their differences. Others were not so anxious for an amiable solution. The "One University Plan," advocated by many University of Texas supporters, called for, among other things, consolidation of the College with the University and its removal as soon as practicable to Austin. Also in the plan was conversion of A&M buildings and properties into a state hospital for the insane.

Naturally, the College reacted. The Corps of Cadets submitted a petition, as did the Farmers' Congress and various alumni groups. It appeared that the Battle of the Universities was about to be renewed. The battle, however, ended before it began, in another temporary stalemate and postponement. The whole scene would be replayed again at the opening of the next legislative session.

New troubles at A&M added greater intensity to the consolidation movement, just at the time when the critical legislative session of 1913 was getting un-

Robert Teague Milner was president of the College from 1908 and 1913. Courtesy Texas A&M University Archives.

Charles Puryear, professor, first dean of the College, and a member of the faculty between 1889 and 1940, provided much of the initiative and guidance for early twentieth-century progress at A&M. Courtesy Texas A&M University Archives.

derway. Hazing was again making headlines. A University of Texas student was shot and killed in a hazing incident. Governor Colquitt attributed the fires at A&M in 1911 and 1912 to incendiary origins. An A&M student drowned trying to swim the Brazos. Neither the A&M fires nor the swimming tragedy had anything to do with hazing, but both events attracted unfavorable attention in the press.

Hazing and a general feeling of unrest among the student body combined to produce a crisis. In 1913, faculty efforts to control hazing and maintain discipline touched off another student strike. Twenty-seven cadets were dismissed. Members of the freshman and sophomore classes protested, presented a petition, and asked for reinstatement of the students concerned. The faculty held fast, dismissed 466 petition signers, and the strike began.

The legislature passed a no-hazing bill. Bad publicity caused Texans to take a second look at the pending consolidation question. A&M administrators extended amnesty to its dismissed students and required the 466 petition signers to take an iron-clad pledge to abide by all rules and abstain from hazing.

The A&M Alumni Association mailed circular letters in opposition to the proposed constitutional amendment to be voted on by the people of Texas. In

July, 1913, the amendment was defeated at the polls.

A 1914 University of Texas proposal asked A&M to join in urging the Thirty-fourth Legislature to enact a proposed constitutional amendment which would, among other things, make A&M an independent college, allow legislative appropriations and tax levies for capital construction, and specify the interests of A&M in the permanent fund, "if any."

A&M made a counterproposal: equal division of the permanent fund and equal division of a tax levy. University regents asked for another meeting in 1914. A&M directors extended a meeting invitation later in the year. Fencing continued between Austin and College Station, and the Thirty-fourth Legislature approved a proposed amendment which, for the most part, reflected 1913 agreements.

Meanwhile, a quiet revolution was occurring on the A&M campus. Agriculture and engineering studies were attaining strength and public recognition. The term "Aggie," as mentioned earlier, is a relatively modern one. Certainly, in almost any period of the

Cadets learned early agricultural techniques in the greenhouse, 1903. Courtesy Texas A&M University Archives.

Cumbersome by today's standards, this tractor was a mechanical marvel around 1913. Courtesy Texas A&M University Archives.

A 1902 artillery group poses at the ready. Courtesy Texas A&M University Archives.

College's history before or after 1900, it would not properly identify the major effort at Texas A&M. A far more descriptive term would be "Engineers."

The curricula of the 1870s offered A&M students a strong foundation in engineering and nothing in agriculture. Surveying, descriptive geometry, mechanics, and drawing were offered for juniors. Seniors studied shades, shadows, and perspective, descriptive astronomy, railroad surveying, strength of materials, arches, framing, free-hand drawing, mapping, sketches of tools, and designs for the component parts of machines, bridges, and other structures.

During the early years, the College gave little more than lip service to agriculture. In the academic year 1880–81, 18 percent of the students were enrolled in agriculture as opposed to 83 percent in engineering. There was, at the time, a general aversion

on the part of A&M students to anything smacking of farm labor. A great many of them had grown up on farms, and their ambition was to get off the land, not back to it.

Engineering, although apparently more popular than agriculture, also suffered during the early eighties. The great emphasis on "practical" training forced engineers away from the drawing board and into the workshops. For a while, engineering was synonymous with woodworking and blacksmithing.

The later years of the decade brought a clear upsurge in agricultural enrollments. In 1890, the College for the first time graduated as many agricultural students as engineers. Three years later, for the first and only time in its history, A&M graduated more agricultural than engineering students—eight for agriculture, seven for engineering.

Turn-of-the-century studies more accurately reflected the needs of the hour. There were separate civil engineering and physics departments and a new department called electrical engineering. Engineers from Texas A&M produced much of the know-how to bring about the industrial development of Texas and the South.

Throughout most of its existence, A&M has largely been something other than an agricultural school, despite the popular connotation of the term "Aggie." Texas A&M graduates became businessmen, teachers, engineers, soldiers, veterinarians, and professionals as well as agriculturists.

Whether it has played a dominant role or not, agriculture has done a great deal toward maintaining the growth and programs of the College. The advent of the Agricultural Experiment Station in 1888 had

The regiment around *1910. Courtesy Texas A&M University Archives.*

There was plenty to learn about the relatively new invention called the automobile. *Courtesy Texas A&M University Archives.*

much to do with A&M's survival and progress. It helped convince the public not only of the efficacy of "scientific agriculture" and agricultural education, but of the value and repute of the entire College.

The Experiment Station made it easier to sell farmers on the value of scientific farming and, quite often, actively helped farmers solve their problems. By 1893, it had issued a total of twenty-five Experiment Station bulletins on such topics as the causes of alfalfa root rot and the chemical composition of grasses and forage plants. Five years later the station's mailing list totaled twelve thousand names. A substation at Beeville was established in 1895 and another at Alvin in 1898. By 1930, there were sixteen substations in widespread parts of the state.

The greatest accomplishments of the Texas Agricultural Experiment Station research program include such breakthroughs as the elimination of Texas fever, the development of Sudan grass, the control of root rot in cotton, and the control of loin disease in cattle. The massive amounts of technical information and personal services provided Texas and U.S. farmers have an inestimable dollar value.

Texas A&M became a strategic catalyst in the inception of the idea of cooperative agricultural extension work. Seaman A. Knapp's demonstration farm work, the county-agent system, the corn clubs which developed into the 4-H Club program, and an organized agricultural extension program had an early beginning in Texas and developed after 1905 under the auspices of Texas A&M. The College had a fully developed agricultural extension program operating under the United States Department of Agriculture by 1912, before the passage of the historic Smith-Lever Act of 1914, which established agricultural extension as a nationwide service program.

By 1910, Texas A&M offered eight degree programs, and only one of these, agriculture, was unrelated to engineering. In addition to agriculture, degree programs included architecture, chemical engineering, agricultural engineering, civil engineering, electrical engineering, mechanical engineering, and textile engineering. James C. Nagle became the first dean of the School of Engineering by action of the board of directors on November 11, 1911.

In 1913, Texas A&M formed the Texas Engineering Experiment Station to "supply information to the general public through printed bulletins, and to make important investigations in the field of engineering."

Thus, A&M was not far behind the University of Illinois and Iowa State College in this area. The first such facilities were begun at those institutions in 1903.

Despite the historic preference of A&M students for engineering, that curriculum also struggled for a place in the sun. Before 1915, engineers received no direct federal assistance comparable to that provided for the agricultural program. Engineers, however, had one advantage over their "farmer" colleagues—their vocation was clearly in harmony with the spirit of the times. The industrial and scientific revolution was blossoming in America. There were far more cash-paying jobs for engineers than for farmers. And the real demand for trained engineers was just beginning.

William Bennett Bizzell became president of A&M in 1914. His tenure marked the beginning of one of the most successful administrations in the College's history. During Bizzell's term, Texas A&M received larger appropriations for building construction than the total received since its founding. If Sul Ross brought A&M out of its dark ages, Bizzell took it into the modern era.

In 1913, the board helped launch A&M into contemporary times by bringing "movies" to campus.

In 1914, the position of athletic director was created in response to the growing role of organized sports on the campus. Charles B. Moran had joined A&M as football coach four years before and played a big role in making the College football-conscious. The 1914 *Longhorn* boasted that between 1902 and 1913, the "Farmers" had won seventy-three football games, lost eighteen, and tied four. It was an ideal way to view the record, as the 1913 team itself lost more games in one season than previous teams had managed to lose in the past four.

The baseball team won ninety-six games, lost fifty-four, and tied four between 1904 and 1913. The A&M track team won first in the state meet in both 1910 and 1911.

The 1914–15 football squad lost only one game—to the Haskell Indians. Cadets defeated Texas Christian University 40–0, Louisiana State University 63–9, Rice Institute 32–7, Oklahoma A&M 24–0, and Mississippi State University 14–7. In 1915, the A&M eleven lost only to Rice and Mississippi A&M. And, for the first time since 1911, A&M played the University of Texas. A&M won, 13–0.

In 1915, cadets took great pride in being part of a military outfit. Uniforms were still the traditional gray

William Bennett Bizzell (*1914–25*) presided over a period of great achievement at Texas A&M, in both peace and war. *Courtesy Texas A&M University Archives.*

Always plenty of passengers. Note that the sign at the station reads simply "College." Courtesy Texas A&M University Archives.

In *1910*, a gasoline-operated trolley began making the run between Bryan and College Station. The trolley converted to electricity in *1915*. Courtesy Texas A&M University Archives.

The Illyrians, a drama society, present an all-male production of Twelfth Night in *1911*. Courtesy Texas A&M University Archives.

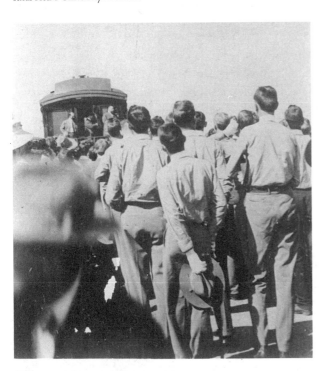

Cadets crowd to get a view of President William Howard Taft as his train stops at College Station. Courtesy Texas A&M University Archives.

with black stripes on the trousers and black braid on the blouse front and cuffs. It was easy to know whom to salute. Cadet officers wore black and gold cord on their academy-style hats. Freshmen wore a blue cord, sophomores yellow, and juniors red; most seniors had officer rank. Hazing still got out of hand now and then, but seniors made strong efforts to keep things

under control. A hazing report from a cadet officer was enough to have a cadet dismissed from school. Nevertheless, midnight track meets, pranks, and some paddling occurred. There was also a great deal of esprit de corps.

Big-time football had arrived by 1916. The Thanksgiving game against Texas University at Austin drew "the largest crowd at an athletic contest south of the Mason-Dixon line." The stands were filled with 15,800 fans and receipts totaled around $21,000. It was such a good season A&M paid its old obligations, met all current expenses, and made needed improvements.

A&M also "cleaned up" its athletics, reported Andrew Love, chairman of the Faculty Athletic Committee, and it could never again be said that "A&M teams are composed of men that are not gentlemen and that have been coached to play dirty, under-hand games."

When "Charlie" Moran left, E. H. W. ("Jigger") Harlan from Princeton became head coach. He stayed for the 1915 and 1916 seasons and was replaced by Dana X. Bible.

President Bizzell played an important role in putting A&M intercollegiate athletics on a well-organized, "businesslike" basis. Part of this effort involved organization of the Southwest Athletic Conference in 1914. Texas A&M was a charter member.

A tradition of athletic rivalry between A&M and the University of Texas began on the gridiron, and the political game between the two schools continued unabated.

Coach Moran's baseballers of *1910* had a less than enviable record of seven wins, nine losses, and one tie. Team members, who cannot be individually identified, included: G. F. H. Bittle (captain), Eugene A. Eversberg, Walter S. Moore, Clifton M. Henderson, Walter W. Whipkey, David M. Puckett, George Simmons, Thomas E. Thompson, Calvin P. Dodson, Edwin P. Arneson, Caesar ("Dutch") Hohn, Arland L. Ward (manager). *Courtesy Texas A&M University Archives.*

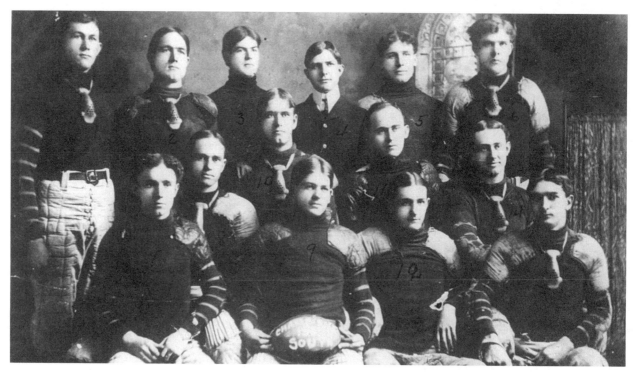

The first A&M football team to defeat the University of Texas, *1902.* Left to right from top: Ray Ridenhower (sub guard), Jud Neff (left guard), Bob Deware (field), James Platt (coach), Joseph Benjamin (right guard), B. Simpson (left tackle), Josh Sterns (right end), James Worthing (center), Jim Pirie (sub field), George Hope (right tackle), William Beihare (quarter), Tom Blake (captain), Jim Davis (left end), Miles Carpenter (left end). *Courtesy Texas A&M University Archives.*

Around the turn of the century, cadets marched everywhere—to classes, mess, assembly, chapel. Courtesy Texas A&M University Archives.

Texas elected a new governor in 1915. "Farmer Jim" Ferguson was not kindly disposed toward higher education, either at the University of Texas or A&M. "It is apparent to any fair-minded person that Texas is today suffering more from a want of under-education of the many than it is from a want of over-education of the few," he said. "There is a real danger of somebody going hog wild about higher education."

In 1915, the legislature authorized a School of Veterinary Medicine for A&M and established a State For-

estry Service. Both actions had a profound effect upon the growth and development of the College.

There were other signs of progress. Athletics were organized and expanded, student enrollment increased considerably, and faculty and staff grew at a rapid rate.

Even while innovative programs were being introduced and the old programs expanded, Texas A&M, like many other colleges across the country, began to feel the effects of war. Germany declared war on France in August, 1914. By September, German armies were

The Corps of Cadets in *1915*, in formation before the new administration building completed in *1914* on the site of Old Main, which burned in *1912*. Courtesy Texas A&M University Archives.

Sunday morning inspection at tent city about *1913*. World War I ended this regular inspection on the campus. Courtesy Texas A&M University Archives.

thirty miles from Paris, and German-Austrian armies were mauling the Russians in the east.

On June 3, 1916, Congress passed the National Defense Act authorizing establishment of Reserve Officer Training Corps programs at qualifying educational institutions. Texas A&M fully embraced the military training program which so thoroughly complemented its military orientation. For the next several years, military training and the war almost overwhelmed the academic aspects of the College. The mark of the military, if it had not been so before, now became an indelible part of A&M's history and tradition.

"...the atmosphere of old A. and M. pervades
this high ceilinged dining room in France
tonight, and its walls have echoed to a 'Chigaroo
garem' and to 'Rough tough, real tuff' in
good old A. and M. style..."

Yanks go over the top during training in World War I. Courtesy U.S. Army.

III.

The War Years

Texas A&M entered the war years essentially a local agricultural and mechanical school, in a world where agricultural and technical training still had to prove itself. It was a military school in a country where military schools were not uncommon. It was different only in that it tried to blend the gentlemanly occupation of the military into the less gentlemanly pursuits of farming and engineering. The Texas A&M College of 1920 bore little resemblance to the A&M of five years before. Previously, the school had little reputation outside its local environs, either for its military, agricultural, or engineering capabilities. It emerged from the war years with a proud and proved record in all three.

Enrollment declined during the war, but soared with the return of peace. The regular session ending in June, 1920, showed 1,902 students on campus—more than double the number enrolled in 1915. Despite the war, physical growth between 1915 and 1920 was equally impressive. The new YMCA building, a three-story hospital, fireproof dairy barn, Guion Hall, and Bizzell Hall were among the projects completed during these years.

The Reserve Officers Training Program had both immediate and long-term effects on A&M. It helped regularize military training and lent it a professional air. More than that, the war helped justify the school's traditional military orientation, a feature that had long been seriously questioned by many Texans.

Texas A&M made every effort to do its part during the war years. In October, 1916, College officials applied to the War Department for permission to establish a senior ROTC program. The application was approved, and the program was funded by Congress and fully instituted at A&M by September, 1917. ROTC participation was mandatory for all freshmen and sophomores. All students could receive uniforms from the federal government, and juniors and seniors who elected to continue in the ROTC received monthly allotments and all expenses for summer training. Upon graduation, cadets could be commissioned as reserve army officers and, upon election, as temporary second lieutenants in the regular army.

Regardless of their decision to go into advanced ROTC, all A&M students remained members of the Corps of Cadets and wore the same army uniform. In September, 1917, cadets put away the old gray and black uniforms that had been in use for over forty years and donned army khaki and campaign hats.

Anticipating the declaration of war, the A&M faculty, in March, 1917, offered the entire facilities of the College to the federal government for war training purposes. The board ratified the proposal, and A&M became the first college in the United States to take such action.

President Bizzell went to Washington seeking tents, equipment for a cadet cavalry unit, and the assignment of additional army officers to the College.

"September Drill" of 1915 vintage signifies input of freshman "fish" into A&M's educational and military training processes. Courtesy Texas A&M University Archives.

Aggie "Wampus Club" members. Seated, left to right: T. H. Clement, Tom Bittle, Baster Melegard; standing: Henry Foster (son of President Foster), Carey Hutson (son of C.W. Hutson). Courtesy Texas A&M University Archives.

"Retreat," 1917–18. Courtesy University Studios.

On April 6, President Woodrow Wilson announced the declaration of war on Germany. From that day through the academic session in June, 1919, Texas A&M remained on a war footing.

Immediately after the declaration of war, nearly the entire senior class was excused from further duties so they could enter the first officers training school at Camp Funston, Leon Springs, Texas. Other students were enlisting directly into various branches of the service. President Bizzell, upon the urging of the junior class, obtained special permission from the War Department for juniors to attend the school at Leon Springs. The student body was gradually being depleted. Those who remained were on a wartime schedule, for, while class work continued, the stress was now on drilling and military exercises.

By June, there were virtually no seniors left on campus, and officials decided to hold commencement at Leon Springs. Seniors in good standing—irrespective of their failure to complete classwork for the session—were awarded diplomas.

In September, 1917, 112 men of the Depot Company "K," U.S. Army Signal Corps, arrived at A&M for training. A&M's electrical engineering faculty conducted the technical instructions. An intensified training program for practical auto and truck mechanics began in April, 1918, and by September of that year, the course had produced 1,731 mechanics for the army. That same year, the Signal Corps established on the campus a course in meteorology designed to train weather observers for the armed forces. Military training courses on campus in 1918 ranged from auto and radio mechanics to horse shoeing. By September, A&M had trained 3,648 soldiers in various skills.

War training, of course, was in addition to the regular academic schedule. Academics understandably suffered during this time, and students "had their minds and hearts in the war; the quest for knowledge was forgotten."

It was just as well, perhaps, for the faculty was geared for war, too. Many had volunteered for service, and others were working for the war effort in governmental jobs or private industry.

In the fall of 1918, the Student Army Training Corps (SATC) supplanted the regular ROTC program. SATC was open to all men over eighteen who planned to go to college. They were allowed to register for the draft and were immediately inducted into the army as SATC privates. At school they received army pay, and qualified students were selected for officers training schools. Without SATC, academic work on many campuses would have come to a virtual standstill. For in September, the draft age was lowered to eighteen.

Field artillery standing gun drill, *1917–18*. Courtesy Texas A&M University Archives.

The famous Aggie "T" of *1917* vintage. Courtesy Texas A&M University Archives.

"Housecleaning time" at Ross Hall. Courtesy Texas A&M University Archives.

The first aerial view of the campus, 1917. Courtesy Texas A&M University Archives.

World War I campus bayonet practice. Courtesy Texas A&M University Archives.

There was a serious housing crisis. Temporary barracks were built. President Bizzell appealed for help to the citizens of Bryan. Tents, an old standby at A&M, were erected again on the campus.

The influenza epidemic that was sweeping the nation took its toll at College Station. Students, faculty members, and army personnel were struck down. As many as five or six persons were dying each night. The local undertakers ran out of caskets and started using long wicker baskets for the dead.

Saddling instruction, *1917–18*. Courtesy Texas A&M University Archives.

The A&M Infantry ROTC performs setting-up exercises, *1917–18*. Courtesy Texas A&M University Archives.

Map-making was one of the wartime courses taught at A&M. Courtesy Texas A&M University Archives.

One of the many trees around the A&M drill field dedicated to Aggies who gave their lives in World War I. Photograph by Jerry C. Cooper.

One by-product of the war was the assignment of the first woman faculty member to the traditionally all-male College. Mrs. Wanda M. Farr joined A&M as a biology instructor, and the Bryan newspaper commented, "Scarcity of available men make it necessary to select a woman to take the work, but she is said to be fit for her position." Mrs. Farr, a graduate of Ohio State University, did graduate study at Columbia University and taught at Kansas State College before coming to Texas A&M. Her appointment set a precedent.

The war generated among Texas A&M faculty, students, and alumni a great sense of patriotism, purpose, and fraternity. From "somewhere in France," on November 10, 1918, the day before the armistice was signed, a group of A&M soldiers wrote the editor of the *Alumni Quarterly*:

Dear Brother Alumnus:

If you could look in on us tonight and forget where we were, you might easily imagine it a gathering of some of the old boys in the College Mess, except that our uniforms are of olive drab instead of cadet blue. The cloth is as white, the silver as gleaming and the food as good as at some of the special treats that Bernard Sbisa used to set for us. In fact, the atmosphere of old A. and M. pervades this high ceilinged dining room in France tonight, and its walls

The World War I Memorial at A&M's West Gate. Photograph by Jerry C. Cooper.

Governor Neff presides at the unveiling of a monument to the A&M men who gave their lives in World War I. Courtesy Texas A&M University Archives.

Cadets on the road to Bryan in November, 1919, celebrate the Armistice ending World War I. Courtesy Texas A&M University Archives.

have echoed to a "Chigaroo garem" and to "Rough tough, real tuff" in good old A. and M. style. Possibly the waiters think we have gone crazy or that perhaps we have heard through some private channel that the Kaiser has committed suicide. At any rate they do not understand "Zese droll Americaines" but you would and you'd know how good we feel to be here together . . .

. . . Now we will pledge A. and M. and you and all our brothers over there and over here in the wine of France.

Texas A&M was justifiably proud of its contributions to the war effort. It had trained thousands of men for the armed forces in special fields of service, and it had sent most of its able-bodied men to war. Fully one-half of the men who had graduated from A&M since it was established participated as soldiers in the war. Large numbers of the others entered government service. By March, 1918, Texas A&M had a larger percentage of its graduates in service (37.5 percent) than any other college or university in the United States. By September, President Bizzell reported that 49 percent of the all-time graduates of A&M were in military service. A&M graduates included 2 brigadier generals, 7 colonels, 12 lieutenant colonels, 52 majors, 173 captains, 456 first lieutenants, and 530 second lieutenants. A number of men were decorated for bravery. Several received promotions on the field of battle for heroism and unusual discretion under trying and dangerous conditions.

Forty-nine A&M soldiers died in service. Of these, four received the croix de guerre posthumously, six were awarded the Distinguished Service Cross, and two were cited by the commanding officers for personal valor.

In the early morning hours of November 11, 1918, College Station residents were aroused by repeated blasts of the power-plant whistle. The armistice had been signed. The war was over. There was great jubilation on the campus. And some regret among those who knew they would never get to France, now.

Demobilization was as sudden and chaotic as mobilization had been. The SATC began disbanding almost immediately. Confusion reigned on the campus. Very little was accomplished from November 11 through late December. After Christmas, President Bizzell announced that classes would be resumed and that two special terms would be scheduled to allow students to complete their academic studies.

The fall term of 1919 opened on a more normal basis. But there was a difference. Many of the students were veterans. All felt older and more experienced. Texas A&M had changed. It was a war school, with an earned and honorable military reputation. There was greater purpose and dedication, a greater spirit of fraternity. And the military aspects of the College had assumed a larger role.

On May 4, 1919, the bronze statue of Lawrence Sullivan Ross was unveiled. Oak trees were planted on campus to commemorate the war dead. Plans began to formulate for an Alumni Memorial Stadium to be dedicated to those who had given their lives in World War I.

Along with the military honors, Texas A&M achieved a higher degree of fulfillment in her technical specialties of agriculture and engineering during the war years. The critical shortage of engineers during the war provided its own justification for A&M's efforts. Agriculturists convinced farmers and the general public, perhaps for the first time, of the very real necessity for scientific farming, research, and extension. One of the great marvels of World War I was the enormous increase in production by American farmers.

World War I was a distinct milestone in the history of A&M. The society that emerged from the conflict was a society of producers, engineers, scientists, and agriculturists. It was the world for which Texas A&M had been originally designed.

*"The Great War brought change to A&M,
and the College assumed new goals,
new directions . . . things would never be the same . . ."*

An A&M "shopping center," about 1921. Courtesy Texas A&M University Archives.

IV.

Peace, and a New Purpose

A 1919 campus visitor might decide that academic life was finally returning to normalcy at Texas A&M. Not so. The Great War had made its mark, and the College would never again be the same. And while the changes were subtle ones, they were, at the same time, very real and meaningful.

Both the students and the College assumed a new purposefulness. Many of the old doubts and uncertainties about the goals and directions of A&M disappeared in the smoke of war. Veterans brought new ideas and a sense of social responsibility. President Bizzell said there had been a "mental shake-up" in the minds of this new generation—the result of war, automobiles, moving pictures, radio, and "the marvelous mechanical devices of the modern age."

It was a time of experiment and change. New educational theories and approaches came to light, often to the alarm of traditionalists. There were social changes too. Bizzell warned that college students faced unusual distractions in these modern times, that while a career in college should not be a period of "dig, grind, and hard labor," too many diversions "fritter" away the student's time.

The greatest diversion of the 1920s appeared to be the automobile. Many believed that this new marvel was more a curse than a blessing and that it was the root cause of the new sexual license, changing social values, climbing divorce rates, and other unsettling influences. To combat this hazard, President Bizzell and the faculty banned the ownership and use of automobiles by students.

The nation in general was suffering change and contradiction. Prohibition vied with the speakeasy. Isolation seemed less than realistic in a world of growing internationalism. The Ku Klux Klan, lynchings, and gangsterism confused a people previously comfortable in self-righteous security. The Model A puffed along roads built for wagons, and airplanes flew the skies previously reserved for birds.

At College Station, returning veterans refused to have anything to do with military training and were exempted from participation. Paradoxically, it was these men who gave the military program at Texas A&M its outstanding reputation. Because of them, the program expanded rapidly in the 1920s.

After the war, the public made enormous demands on the nation's colleges and universities. Enrollment at Texas A&M in 1919 was 50 percent greater than in any previous year. That enrollment growth continued throughout the twenties and thirties. President Bizzell pointed out that for each 250 students added to the main campus, approximately nine additional teachers, one dormitory, one laboratory, and enlarged dining and classroom facilities were required.

Still, in the face of these new demands on higher education, there was a widespread sentiment against public spending. From 1918 through the end of his administration, Bizzell appealed for needed appropria-

The Texas A&M campus, about 1930. Courtesy University News Service.

tions. There was a steady rise in the cost of living. Private business and industry tempted the academic world with higher salaries. Of the male students who finished high school in Texas in 1923, one-third enrolled at A&M. The College was growing at the rate of six hundred students a year. In 1923, three hundred students were sleeping in tents.

A&M survived fiscal retrenchment and swelling enrollments, but it took great effort. President Bizzell can be given great credit for keeping the College on an even keel during these times. Few college or university presidents of that era were better salesmen for higher education.

A new Battle of the Universities began between 1915 and 1917. Governor Ferguson had his own opinions on the role of higher education and particularly

The Aggieland Inn, about *1920*. Courtesy Texas A&M University Archives.

Cadet William A. Tolson sits at the controls of Station 5YA, which became WTAW in *1922*. Believed to be a first was the play-by-play radio broadcast of the A&M-Texas football game in *1919*. Courtesy Texas A&M University Archives.

President Bizzell enjoys a football game at Kyle Field in the twenties. Courtesy Texas A&M University Archives.

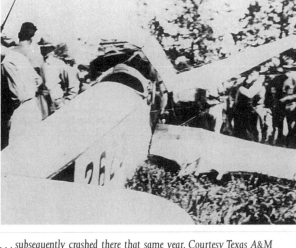

A winged visitor at the A&M campus in 1921—an army airplane temporarily stationed at the College . . . Courtesy Texas A&M University Archives.

. . . subsequently crashed there that same year. Courtesy Texas A&M University Archives.

on the manner in which the University of Texas conducted its business. He attempted to dismiss a number of the University's faculty members in 1917. When the board of regents balked, he tried, unsuccessfully, to revamp that body. He vetoed an appropriations bill for the University of Texas and the Medical Branch at Galveston but, peculiarly, left A&M alone. His fight was primarily with the University.

More troubles ensued between Ferguson, the people, and the legislature, and late in 1917, he was impeached and suspended from office. Lieutenant Governor William P. Hobby took over as acting governor, and the legislature took a closer look at the needs of Texas' institutions of higher learning. Action against Ferguson and proceedings of the Thirty-fifth Legislature set the course for the University of Texas and Texas A&M: schools would have greater control of their own destinies, and, if there was a primary guiding body for these institutions, it would be the legislature itself, and not the governor.

Legislative committee recommendations supported most of the objectives of A&M administrators, including separation of A&M from the University of Texas, equitable division of the permanent university fund, a tax for improvements at all state institutions of higher learning, and rejection of the lingering issue of a coequal agricultural and mechanical college in West Texas.

Again, however, a constitutional amendment failed to bring about separation, and it would be another decade before this long-standing issue was settled.

Mechanized artillery and the cavalry join forces on campus in 1920. Courtesy Texas A&M University Archives.

West Texas, however, did obtain its new college. And, rather than being confined to strict agricultural and mechanical subjects, Texas Technological College in Lubbock received a broader educational mandate.

Changes also widened the scope of higher education at Texas A&M. Admission requirements were raised, and teaching standards were improved. Compulsory physical training was initiated, and a course in Americanism was introduced. The curriculum was broadened to include such subjects as industrial education and agricultural administration. Graduate courses in agriculture, architecture, civil engineering, and other fields were offered. By 1920, the College maintained twenty-nine academic departments. Origination of the

Cadets leaving Sbisa Hall, about *1920*. Courtesy Texas A&M University Archives.

The *80*-piece Aggie Band of *1924*, on the way to becoming the famous *340*-man Fighting Texas Aggie Band of today. Courtesy Texas A&M University Archives.

Cadets dining in Sbisa Hall, about *1925*. Courtesy University Studio.

President Thomas O. Walton (left) and Francis Marion Law, president of
the board of directors, at the Semi-Centennial Celebration in *1926*.
Courtesy Texas A&M University Archives.

Irene ("Mom") Claghorn nursed thousands of Aggies at Texas A&M over
a span of nearly forty years. Courtesy Texas A&M University Archives.

Aggies never tire of "sawing Varsity's horns off." Photograph by Mike Kellett. Courtesy Texas A&M University Photographic Services.

Silver Taps ... the Twelfth Man ... Aggie Muster ... traditions which grew from laughter, pain, and pride line up before us in orderly fashion on yesterday's parade ground ...

Construction of the Academic Building began in *1912*. Built on the ashes of Old Main, Academic guards the past, serves the present, and contemplates the future. Courtesy Texas A&M University Photographic Services.

The Joe H. Reynolds Medical Sciences Building, completed in *1983*, represents a new area of service by the University.
Courtesy Texas A&M University Photographic Services.

Oceanography-Meteorology Building and the System Administration Building. Courtesy Texas A&M University Photographic Services.

The Aggie yells show the students' spirit and love for Texas A&M. Photograph by James Lyle. Courtesy Texas A&M University Photographic Services.

Whipping out—the Corps of Cadets has been central to campus life since the opening of the College in 1876. Photograph by Jean Wulfson. Courtesy Texas A&M University Photographic Services.

The strange and the familiar come together ... the fantasies and dreams of one age become the shapes and sounds of another ...

The president's home—ready for holiday celebrations. Courtesy Texas A&M University Photographic Services.

C. C. Krueger Hall and E. J. Mosher Hall, both women's dormitories. Courtesy Texas A&M University Photographic Services.

J. Earl Rudder Center. Courtesy Texas A&M University Photographic Services.

Puryear Hall. Courtesy Texas A&M University Photographic Services.

And from here it seems that what is,
ever was ... that the Texas A&M
of today could surely have had
no small beginnings ...
But there was a yesterday ...

Joe C. Richardson, Jr., Petroleum Engineering Building.
Courtesy Texas A&M University Photographic Services.

"Contemplate"—a thing students often do. Photograph by Mike Kellett. Courtesy Texas A&M University Photographic Services.

Professor of history Betty Unterberger offers Texas Aggies a global perspective, something urgently needed for the twenty-first century. Courtesy Texas A&M University Photographic Services.

The campus as seen looking north from Rudder Tower in 1976. Photograph by Jim Bones.

The "new" Guion Assembly Hall around *1921*. The service flag on stage was dedicated to Texas A&M by act of Congress in commemoration of Aggies who served and died in World War I. The outside stars represent those in service; the center group of stars represents those who died in service. Courtesy Texas A&M University Archives.

The sign above A&M's West Gate proudly announces Aggie successes. Courtesy University Studio.

On the fiftieth anniversary of A&M, in *1926*, the academic procession marches down Military Walk to Guion Hall. Courtesy Texas A&M University Archives.

"Hollywood shacks" replaced tent city on campus after World War I. This form of temporary housing remained in use until *1931*. Courtesy Texas A&M University Archives.

Final Review in *1928*. Seniors mark the end of undergraduate days and pass on their authority to the junior class. Courtesy Texas A&M University Archives.

The *Agricultural Building*, built in *1922*, was renovated in *1995* to house the department of history and other programs. *Courtesy Texas A&M University Archives.*

This *1928* bonfire heap was typical of many Aggie bonfires—it contained a little of everything. *Courtesy Texas A&M University Archives.*

The *Aggie bonfire has long been a cherished tradition. Courtesy Texas A&M University Archives.*

School of Vocational Teaching and creation of the School of Arts and Sciences in 1924 marked the beginning of a broadening of the A&M academic orientation away from the pure applied technical training in agriculture and engineering that had been the dominant feature of the College since the 1890s. Also indicative of Texas A&M's new educational role was the establishment of the graduate school in 1924, offering master's degrees in twelve subjects.

There were more visible changes, too. A new cadet uniform appeared in 1920. The Aggieland Inn was completed in 1925, and construction of Kyle Field began in 1927. Despite its newness, the modern Texas A&M College was firmly rooted in its academic principles and purposes. It was first and foremost an agricultural and mechanical college. For at least the next thirty years, the College expanded and developed upon the foundations it had established by 1925.

Another A&M tradition survived into the modern era. The Senate began an investigation of hazing in 1921 and called upon students, parents, and alumni to

help suppress the more undesirable aspects of this practice. A new antihazing pledge came into being, but hazing again caught the public eye in 1924.

There were, certainly, practices that could in reality be called nothing more nor less than "hazing." But many of the student activities were simply part of the mysteries of becoming an Aggie. As the Senate investigation concluded in 1921, rather than being brutal, this kind of life generated among students a "spirit of love, loyalty and dedication" for the school and for the Corps of Cadets.

In May, 1925, President Bizzell resigned to become president of the University of Oklahoma. The qualities that endeared him to Texans and Texas A&M endeared him also to Oklahomans and the University of Oklahoma. When he retired from that position in 1941 at the age of sixty-five, after sixteen years of service, he was recognized as one of the University of Oklahoma's most able and productive presidents.

During his years at Texas A&M, the College had

matured into a full-grown, accepted, and accredited institution. Texas A&M had entered the age for which it was designed and conceived. The modern era demanded production—production of cotton, corn, wheat, hogs, oil, textiles, furniture, houses, buildings, and factories. The College promised and delivered the farmers, vocational teachers, engineers, and craftsmen who could turn the wheels of American industry. Texas A&M produced soldiers who helped defend the American way of life in the next great war to come. It moved forward with a new zeal, dedication, and purpose. And, to some extent, with a narrowing vision of what tomorrow might bring, it lost itself for a while in the business of producing the magic cornucopia of today.

"There were advantages and disadvantages to being a branch of Texas A&M. Both the fortunes and misfortunes of the parent were shared by the child ..."

A student at Prairie View participates in equipment testing.
Courtesy Texas A&M University Archives.

V.

Growing, Branching Out

The Texas A&M College System, as it was called from 1948 to 1963, began to develop even before A&M College opened its doors for business. The "system" included branch colleges at Prairie View, Arlington, and Stephenville. The Texas Legislature established a branch "for the benefit of colored youths" at Prairie View, by Act of August 14, 1876. In 1917, two "junior agricultural, mechanical and industrial" colleges, one at Arlington and another at Stephenville, were established under the auspices of the Texas A&M Board of Directors.

There were advantages and disadvantages to being a branch of Texas A&M. Both the fortunes and misfortunes of the parent were shared by the child. Each branch, however, has been allowed to seek its own identity and, in many ways, to succeed, fail, and grow in its own particular fashion.

The Prairie View A&M College of Texas, A&M's oldest branch, until contemporary times was the only public institution of higher learning for African Americans in Texas. Its academic history has reflected all the nuances of Southern politics and society. It has not only an academic history and a Texas history, but a black history as well—part of the history of the black man in what, for the most part, was a white man's world.

The site selected for Prairie View was a tract of land known as Alta Vista, near Hempstead, Texas. When the school opened in March, 1878, only eight students enrolled. Like its parent institution, the new college got off to a slow start. While enrollment at A&M grew, however, attendance at Alta Vista declined. In January, 1879, a visiting delegation from the Sixteenth Legislature found the principal of the school, Professor Minor, "but no colored youths seeking instruction." They concluded, "there is no demand for higher education among the blacks." In truth it appears that black students shared the same views as white students at Texas A&M—few were highly motivated to leave the farm so they could study farming in order to return to the farm again.

Several alternate plans for Alta Vista were considered, but in 1879, the legislature established the "Normal School at Prairie View for preparation and training of colored teachers." The school opened in October, 1879. Sixteen students enrolled, but the number grew to sixty-four before the end of the term.

Prairie View A&M between 1878 and 1946 was a separate but unequal institution. The greatest objective of its leaders was continually to upgrade the school and to accommodate the special needs of black citizens, while trying to avoid a confrontation with the white power structure. It was their goal to make the institution a separate but equal haven of learning.

Like the main campus in College Station, Prairie View in the nineteenth century had no adequate water supply and needed wagons, implements, and more money. There were less tangible but equally disturb-

Students leave the Prairie View Memorial Center. Courtesy Texas A&M University Archives.

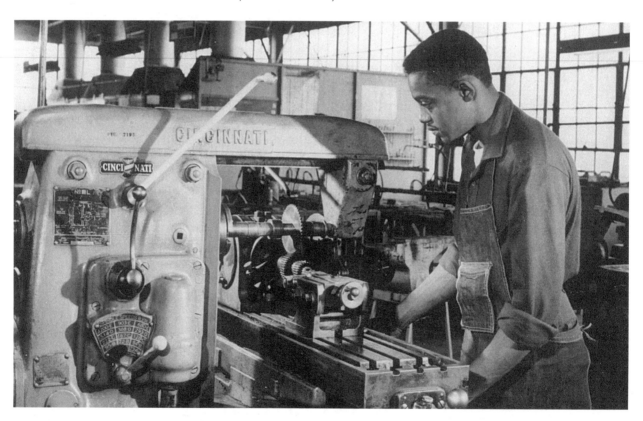

A wide variety of engineering and vocational courses prepares the Prairie View student for a career. Courtesy Texas A&M University Archives.

ing problems as well. The decade of the nineties brought renewed political turbulence and heightened racial antagonisms. Farmers organized a Populist Party to fight the Democrats. Rejuvenated Republicans threatened to ally themselves with the Populists. A new "Force Bill," which white Southerners believed would reinstitute Reconstruction, was being debated in Congress. African Americans were becoming an increasingly important and controversial subject.

In this atmosphere a legislative committee in 1891 reported that Prairie View Normal was "doing excellent work for the colored race" and urged the legislature to give the college as much of an appropriation as possible.

An industrial education course was introduced at Prairie View in 1887. Typesetting, printing, blacksmithing, carpentry, and elementary agriculture were important features of this course. However, Principal L. C. Anderson never lost sight of the goal of the college as a normal school for the training of teachers, who would in turn go out to educate and improve the life of black Texans.

By 1896, however, political storms had settled over Texas. Populists, Republicans, and African Americans were out. The solid Democratic Party was in, and the Democrats felt that Anderson, as a Republican, was no longer suitable as principal. He was replaced by Edward Blackshear, a Democrat.

The legislature changed the institution's name from Prairie View State Normal School to Prairie View State Normal and Industrial College. In 1901, the school began offering a four-year course in "classical and scientific studies." Prairie View held its first commencement in 1904 and needed physical improvements on the campus began to get underway.

Blackshear, Anderson's replacement, also found himself on the losing side of a political fight. His successor, I. M. Terrell, fell before local and faculty hostilities, and Dr. Granville Osborne took the helm in 1918 with the goal of putting Prairie View on a real collegiate basis.

Osborne was an able administrator. He rehabilitated the four-year degree-granting program in 1919, instituted a nursing school, established an ROTC program, raised teacher salaries, established a teacher-training program in vocational agriculture leading to a bachelor of science degree, and instituted a regular B.S. degree in that subject.

But like so many able and aggressive men, Osborne created enemies and pushed many people too hard.

President Bizzell's departure from Texas A&M left Osborne vulnerable to political pressure, and he was dismissed from office.

Willette Banks served as principal of Prairie View from 1926 to 1947. Whatever the school is today is in large measure the product of the work of Banks and his staff and of the successive administration of Edward B. Evans. These two men guided the affairs of the college for four decades, from 1926 through 1965.

Banks built a strong educational program and a strong faculty. He did much with little. He believed the school should extend its education program into the community. Banks helped develop National Youth Administration (NYA) programs on the campus in the thirties, established the Division of Graduate Study, and brought the Army Specialized Training Program to Prairie View. In 1945, he saw the title and function of the institution changed by the state legislature to Prairie View University, authorizing Prairie View to offer all courses offered by the University of Texas. For one "bright moment" Prairie View had a law school and prepared to offer full university curricula.

The new status was short-lived. In 1947, the legislature created Texas Southern University in Houston. The law thus created a university in two parts, and Prairie View again became Prairie View Agricultural and Mechanical College of Texas. It would appear the institution had taken a step backward, but Prairie View had a strong academic foundation and, under the guidance of Edward Bertram Evans, continued its growth and development.

Evans restructured the academic branches of the college to include the Schools of Agriculture, Arts and Sciences, Home Economics, Engineering, Industrial Education and Technology. Numerous physical additions were made to the campus, including a $1 million Memorial Student Center, a $2 million Science Building, and a $1.5 million Health and Physical Education Building. The college was accredited by the Southern Association of Colleges and Secondary Schools in 1958.

Evans retired in 1966 and was followed by Dr. J. M. Drew, who in turn was succeeded by Dr. Alvin I. Thomas. In 1973, the Texas legislature again gave Prairie View "university" status, designating it Prairie View A&M University.

Over the years, the association between Prairie View and Texas A&M has been cordial and beneficial to both institutions. There has, however, been some disagreement over Texas A&M's stewardship. The 1932

Joint Legislative Committee report strongly criticized some practices, stating mainly that A&M had failed to understand some of the elementary principles of black education and that it had dictated nearly every policy and procedure of the Prairie View State Normal and Industrial College. Did Texas A&M saddle Prairie View with its own identity, as the report stated? If the committee's recommendation toward "practical training" was the correct path for Prairie View as the only institution of higher learning for African Americans in Texas, then, indeed, A&M was clearly in the wrong.

Prairie View began in the shadow of Reconstruction, when black education was a new thing and when, under New South doctrine, the African American was to be "uplifted and civilized." With the advent of a more progressive era, black education remained separate, but there was a conscious stirring for equality. Black schools should teach black students what white schools taught white students, not something less. Blackshear, Osborne, and Banks worked for a measure of equality within the framework of separation—admittedly without great success, but with an eye toward tomorrow. Contrary to that purpose, the legislative report of 1932 would have converted Prairie View into a vocational, trades, "general purpose" school for African Americans, rather than a full collegiate institution that paralleled the academic standards and purposes of white colleges.

With the advent of the contemporary Civil Rights era, the law—and public opinion—recognized that separate educational facilities are inherently unequal. This marked the beginning of a social revolution and an academic revolution in the affairs of black colleges, whose whole academic and social philosophy had been geared to separation. Integration forced the black colleges to achieve equality whether they sought it or not. Forced into the mainstream of modern education, they are now forced to accept full equality not only in standards, but in academic responsibility. Prairie View has fully accepted this charge.

And what has been the role of Texas A&M in the development of Prairie View? Contrary to the 1932 report, Texas A&M, for the most part, has not dictated either the academic or social standards of that institution. If there has been an official A&M system policy, it has been to leave branches to their own devices, to develop their own strengths and, with help, to overcome their weaknesses. Under such a license Tarleton State University developed.

John Tarleton was a teacher, merchant, and land

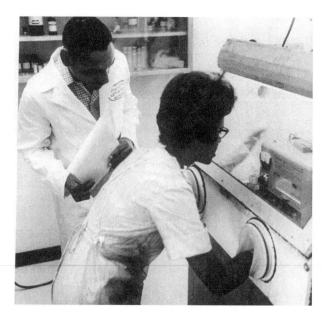

Medical instruction at Prairie View. Courtesy Texas A&M University Archives.

investor. His career as land investor enabled him to amass a great many holdings before his death in 1895. He left his property in Tennessee to found "The John Tarleton Institute" and his holdings in Texas to maintain in the city of Stephenville "The John Tarleton College" for the education of the children of Erath County between the ages of six and eighteen who were of good moral character and unable to educate themselves.

The trustees of Tarleton's estate opened Stephenville College in 1899, with a faculty of four. New rooms were added to the original building between 1902 and 1907, but by 1909, the original endowment was nearly depleted. New bequests helped, and the young college struggled for existence. In 1917, a movement was started to get the state to take over the college as a branch of Texas A&M.

There was some opposition, particularly among Bryan businessmen and Aggie alumni, to Texas A&M branching out. Also, at this time, there was a great deal of support across the state for the establishment of a West Texas A&M College, though A&M supporters opposed creating a "duplicate" A&M in the western part of the state. A legislative investigating committee recommended instead that A&M establish six junior agricultural colleges, including John Tarleton at Stephenville and Grubbs Vocational College at Arlington. At least in part, then, A&M's decision to branch out came as a result of pressure from West Texas to

Aerial view of John Tarleton College at Stephenville in the 1940s. Courtesy Texas A&M University Archives.

establish a "rival" institution. The junior A&M colleges would undermine support for a full-scale West Texas A&M College, while providing useful feeder schools and new regional influence for Texas A&M.

The Thirty-fifth Legislature approved establishment of the Agricultural and Mechanical College of Texas, at Stephenville, in February of 1917. James Cox, who had served as president of Stephenville College since 1913, was named dean of the new branch of A&M.

The college, opened in the fall of 1917, offered the last two years of high school and the first two years of college courses in agriculture, home economics, and the arts and sciences.

James Cox, first dean of John Tarleton Agricultural College, was replaced by J. Thomas Davis in 1919, when Cox became president of Abilene Christian College. Tarleton's curriculum in agriculture and engineering was closely integrated with that at A&M.

Bird's eye view of Grubbs Vocational College, Arlington, Texas. Courtesy Texas A&M University Archives.

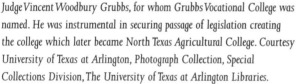

Judge Vincent Woodbury Grubbs, for whom Grubbs Vocational College was named. He was instrumental in securing passage of legislation creating the college which later became North Texas Agricultural College. Courtesy University of Texas at Arlington, Photograph Collection, Special Collections Division, The University of Texas at Arlington Libraries.

Military training was compulsory. Academic growth paralleled that at Texas A&M. While A&M developed along the lines of agriculture, mechanics, sciences, and military science, Tarleton developed along those same lines, with home economics and business administration as distinctive fields.

While Tarleton experienced sustained growth during its early years, it was and is a small college. Since approximately 1950, enrollment has ranged between 2,000 and 3,500. Former president Eugene J. Howell (1945–66) stated that one of the unique qualities and attributes of Tarleton State College, as it is known today, is that it is a small college and retains the personal and comfortable atmosphere of a small college—an atmosphere that has been completely lost on most campuses in contemporary times.

Tarleton is also unique in that it has had only four presidents in its first six decades of existence: James F.

Cox, J. Thomas Davis, Eugene J. Howell, and William Oren Trogdon.

Howell was named dean of Tarleton in 1945 and began his long tenure as dean and president. One of his most important accomplishments, Howell believes, was guiding Tarleton through its postwar growing pains. Over half the students were veterans, and trailers for married students were scattered at various points about the campus. The faculty was thin, and there were only two or three Ph.D's on hand. Howell worked arduously to build the faculty. He succeeded in 1949 in having the name of the college changed to Tarleton State College, reflecting the diminishing role of agriculture in the institution's studies.

In 1953, Tarleton received legislative approval to become a four-year degree-granting institution, authorized to award the B.A. degree in liberal arts only. Tarleton awarded its first degrees in 1963, won full accreditation from the Southern Association of Colleges and Schools in 1966, and has since been authorized to offer the B.A. in ten additional subjects.

Before his retirement in 1966, Howell presided over considerable expansion on the campus. A new student center, library, athletic field, and an agricul-

The entrance to North Texas Agricultural College, *1923*. Courtesy University of Texas at Arlington, Photograph Collection, Special Collections Division, The University of Texas at Arlington Libraries.

The North Texas Agricultural College, class of *1919*, outside the Administration Building. Courtesy University of Texas at Arlington, Photograph Collection, Special Collections Division, The University of Texas at Arlington Libraries.

ture building were constructed. Two women's dormitories and two men's dormitories were built, and the science building was expanded. Shops and roads were expanded and improved. President Trogdon has continued to improve the academic programs of Tarleton and to expand student services.

Shortly after legislative approval of the Stephenville branch, a bill was passed establishing at "Arlington, Tarrant County, Texas, a junior agricultural, mechanical, and industrial college to be known as Grubbs Vocational College." The citizens of Arlington donated to the state one hundred acres of land and the campus and buildings of the Carlisle Military School, which had ceased operations.

The charter for the college in Arlington provided a broader academic mandate than either Tarleton, Prairie View, or Texas A&M itself. A good literary education was called for, along with a knowledge of agriculture, horticulture, floriculture, stock raising, and domestic arts and sciences. The curricula of both Tarleton and Grubbs were modeled on the lines of the Texas A&M curricula and were intended to dovetail into A&M studies so students could transfer into the advanced college courses at College Station without loss of credits or time. This practice tended to discourage academic diversification at the branches.

By the 1930s, Arlington had become heavily committed to a liberal arts and technical program stemming from student demands. Tarleton, on the other hand, continued an academic program in accord with that of Texas A&M. But unlike A&M, it promoted strong programs in education and the liberal arts.

Each branch—and particularly the Arlington branch—was to have different experiences, different demands, and a different academic orientation from those of Texas A&M.

There was some validity to the 1932 report that stated Texas A&M was imposing something of an academic straitjacket on its branches by its narrow emphasis on agriculture and engineering. The first major building contracts awarded at each of the branches in 1918 were for agricultural buildings. The branches had just joined the A&M system, and agriculture then was the order of the day, not only at A&M, but throughout Texas.

Eventually, the board's overriding policy of self-determination allowed the branches sufficient leeway to develop independently in other academic areas.

Grubbs Vocational School at Arlington, renamed North Texas Junior Agricultural College in 1923, experienced much the same development as Tarleton State College, but on a more intensified scale, especially after World War II. Because of its proximity to the burgeoning metropolitan Dallas-Fort Worth area, Arlington experienced tremendous growth in the forties and fifties. It early became oriented toward liberal arts and engineering, while agriculture languished.

After World War II, Arlington was allowed to broaden its curricula substantially, and like Tarleton to grant degrees and establish a full four-year college offering. In 1949, the legislature changed the name of North Texas Junior Agricultural College to Arlington State College. In 1959, the College was elevated to senior rank.

The Texas Commission on Higher Education led to the establishment of the Coordinating Board, Texas College and University System, which defined the role and scope of Texas institutions of higher education. Arlington State College, availing itself of the prevailing political climate, seized the opportunity offered by reorganization to withdraw from the Texas A&M College System, and in 1965 it became a branch of the University of Texas. The name of the College was changed to the University of Texas at Arlington in 1967.

In 1971, George P. Mitchell donated a 100-acre tract of land on Pelican Island, adjacent to Galveston, to Texas A&M University. The Moody Foundation, also of Galveston, provided construction grants for the development of a new College of Marine Sciences and Maritime Resources. Officially organized by the Texas legislature on September 1, 1971, and renamed the Moody College of Marine Sciences and Maritime Resources in 1972, the new adjunct of the main campus reflected Texas A&M's designation by Congress as a sea grant college. The new campus included the existing Texas Maritime Academy. It began instruction in oceanography and marine sciences and focused on the production of Merchant Marine and Coast Guard officers.

From 1965 until 1993, Texas A&M University and Galveston Cadet Corps students trained aboard the *Texas Clipper*, a 1944 former navy ship, which was replaced by the 373-foot *Chauvenet*. The "Aggie Navy" also includes the *Resolution*, a 470-foot former oil-drilling vessel used in the Ocean Drilling Program that explores the ocean bottom and the evolution of marine life. At first an academic branch of Texas A&M University, the Galveston campus soon developed into an independent degree-granting institution—which became Texas A&M University at Galveston.

Slightly over a quarter of a century later, the "system" doubled from four to eight allied campuses. The Texas Legislature placed Laredo State University, Corpus Christi State University, Texas A&I University in Kingsville, and West Texas State University in Canyon under the Texas A&M University System umbrella. Finally the Texas Legislature approved, effective September 1, 1996, the addition of East Texas State University in Commerce and the (independent) Baylor College of Dentistry in Dallas bringing student enrollment in the Texas A&M University System to over one hundred thousand.

Laredo State became Texas A&M International University, and the other institutions were renamed Texas A&M University-Corpus Christi, West Texas A&M University, and Texas A&M University–Kingsville. While the academic campuses of Texas A&M now stretched from the Panhandle to the Rio Grande and into East Texas, Texas A&M, to be sure, had a long history of service to the people of Texas—services that became increasingly diverse and complex to meet the changing needs of society.

*"Establishing new studies at A&M in those
days called for hardy academic pioneers . . .
fortunately for the College, there were
good men on hand . . ."*

Dr. Mark Francis, founder of veterinary medicine at Texas A&M.
Courtesy Texas A&M University Archives.

VI.

Veterinarians, Foresters, and Broadening Services

The agricultural programs of the university, particularly the Agricultural Extension Service and the Texas Agricultural Experiment Station, have been an integral part of the welfare and growth of Texas' agricultural enterprises for much of the past century. Texas farm and ranch receipts, exceeding $12 billion annually in the 1990s, place Texas second only to California in total receipts. Total Texas agribusiness receipts are estimated to exceed $40 billion annually.

For almost a century veterinary medical doctors trained by the Texas A&M University College of Veterinary Medicine have been essential to the growth and development of the Texas livestock industry. The work by veterinarians in public health services is less recognized, but no less significant. Since its inception in 1915, Texas A&M University has administered the Texas Forest Service. Forestry and the foresters produced by the Department of Forestry are a major component of one of Texas' most important industries. Texas' wood products industry, with sales of $5.6 billion in 1994, is the ninth largest of any state in the nation. Veterinarians, foresters, and county agents have for much of A&M's history extended educational and public services throughout Texas and, indeed, into much of the world.

Veterinary medicine had an early but fitful beginning at Texas A&M. Despite initial difficulties, by 1888 veterinary medicine had become a recognized field of study, supported by its own department—and

staffed by one man. Happily, that man was Dr. Mark Francis. Moving steadily ahead from this humble beginning, by the 1930s the School of Veterinary Medicine claimed to have one of the largest and most successful programs in veterinary medicine in the world. Texas A&M's achievement in this field can be attributed largely to the pioneering work of Mark Francis and a handful of men.

The 1879 curriculum in agriculture included a one-semester course in veterinary science. Studies included the anatomy and physiology of domestic animals, veterinary pathology, and symptoms, prevention, and treatment of the general and epizootic diseases of the domestic animals. Lectures were given on heredity and veterinary materia medica—the preparation and use of the principle medicines in veterinary practices.

The entire agricultural program, including the course in veterinary science, virtually ceased to exist when most of the agricultural students changed to the mechanics course during the first fall that the program was offered. Agricultural field work was less attractive than the shopwork required of engineering students. And, as noted earlier, farming held little interest in those years for young men fresh from the farm.

Charles C. Gorgeson, who joined the faculty in 1879, assumed the duty of teaching veterinary science. He reported that "it is about as impossible to teach

A class in livestock and dairying under Professor A. M. Soule, about 1898. Courtesy Texas A&M University Archives.

A&M agricultural students in 1899 receive a lesson in grasses and crops. Courtesy Texas A&M University Archives.

Veterinary anatomy students and subject, 1893–94. Courtesy Texas A&M University Archives.

practical stock-breeding without live stock as to teach carpentry without tools and shop work." He left A&M in 1883.

Interest in agriculture and veterinary science increased—but slowly. A course in veterinary anatomy was introduced. The first class prepared the skeleton of a horse for instructional purposes, and the skeleton remained in use on the A&M campus for many years.

A combination of factors paved the way for the advent of a serious program in veterinary studies. Farmers and cattlemen became increasingly aware of

the merits and economic value of scientific stock breeding and care. A&M began to win support among members of the Grange, and among Texas farmers and cattlemen in particular, for its agricultural programs. Also, the decade of the eighties marked a crossroads for the Texas livestock industry. A practical barbed wire began to have a great impact on the Texas open-range cattle industry, which reached its zenith with the "fencing wars" of 1887 and 1888. The days of the open range were nearly over. In its place came farmers, crop land, and enclosed pastures.

Instruction in scientific farming in *1900* included the development of improved livestock and studies in crop rotation, soil fertility and chemistry, hybridization, and pest control, but the mechanical revolution in agriculture was slow in coming. These oxen remained in use on the A&M campus for some years after *1900*. Ross Hall is in the background. Courtesy Texas A&M University Archives.

Instruction in livestock judging, pictured here about *1899*, continues to be one of the strong academic programs in Texas A&M's College of Agriculture. Courtesy Texas A&M University Archives.

The first veterinary building was erected in 1902 and served the students until 1929. Courtesy Texas A&M University Archives.

The severe winters of 1885 and 1886, followed by protracted droughts, destroyed hundreds of thousands of cattle in Texas and millions in the northern plains. All these factors contributed to the end of open-range ranching and led to more intensive animal husbandry practices. These practices, in turn, created a greater demand for trained veterinarians. Perhaps most influential in the development of veterinary medicine in Texas was the increasing reluctance of northern states to admit Texas cattle and the hesitancy of northern buyers to purchase Texas cattle because of the Texas tick fever.

The wording of the Hatch Act of March 2, 1887, establishing federally supported Agricultural Experiment Stations, suggests that Texas tick fever, a great concern of the American beef industry, played an important role in the formulation of the legislation. The act calls for "research . . . on the physiology of plants and animals; the diseases to which they are severally subject, with the remedies for the same."

Texas fever and the Hatch Act, then, brought about the establishment of an Agricultural Experiment Station at A&M. Coupled with the advent of more intensive stock raising techniques and a more favorable attitude toward scientific agriculture, these factors combined to bring about the establishment of a comprehensive program in veterinary medicine at Texas A&M in 1888.

On January 25, 1888, A&M Directors recognized the Department of Veterinary Science as one of the eleven branches of the College. In June of that year, Dr. Mark Francis of Ohio was named associate professor of veterinary science and veterinarian of the newly created Experiment Station. This appointment marked the real beginning of A&M's program of veterinary medicine. Francis was not only the first veterinarian at Texas A&M, but he became one of the most notable men in American veterinary history.

Like faculty members in other departments at that time, Francis found facilities at A&M sorely lacking. There were no laboratories or equipment, only a room about 14 x 16 feet that served as office, classroom, and laboratory. At the end of that school year, the adjoining room became vacant and was designated as a veterinary classroom. No further classroom or laboratory facilities were constructed for the next fifteen years.

Francis plunged into the Texas fever problem by interviewing and consulting with cattlemen and public figures, including then governor Lawrence Sullivan Ross. He felt there was merit in the theory that the immunity of southern cattle must indicate the physiological equivalent of an antitoxin in the blood and that a quantity of the blood-serum of these apparently immune cattle could be injected into northern cattle, allowing Texas to import high-grade bulls without discouraging losses.

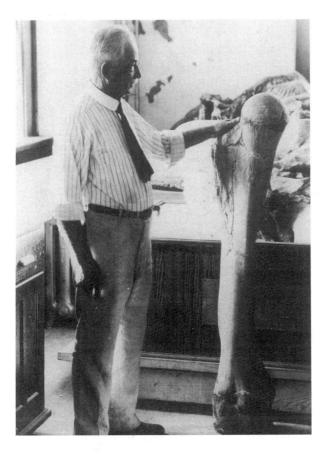

Dr. Mark Francis and one of the prehistoric bones discovered along the Brazos River. Courtesy Texas A&M University Archives.

Dr. Mark Francis (with back to door) and the veterinary lecture room of 1893. Courtesy Texas A&M University Archives.

No funds were available from the legislature for necessary buildings or equipment. Francis felt that the people believed nothing could be done about Texas fever and that experimentation would simply be a waste of money. Finally, about 1900, President Foster managed to obtain $35,000 or $40,000, and Francis proceeded to build a laboratory. The ground floor was to be used for veterinary medicine and the second floor for chemistry. In 1914, a one-story building was assigned as a dissecting room. It remained in use until 1933.

Around 1905, the legislature allowed $125,000 for a suitable building for a proposed School of Veterinary Medicine. Governor Colquitt vetoed the item. Then, Governor James E. ("Farmer Jim") Ferguson, impressed with favorable results obtained in immunizing bulls against Texas fever on his own ranch, told the A&M Board he would approve an appropriation for suitable buildings. The next session of the legislature provided about $100,000, and the building was finally completed in 1918.

Francis' work with Texas fever paid dividends in 1893 and 1894, when transmission was narrowed down to the common Southern tick. A "Device for Dipping Cattle to Destroy Ticks" was carefully detailed in the Texas Agricultural Experiment Station bulletin that reported Francis' findings on the tick itself. The discovery that the tick transmitted Texas fever was the key to the problem of how to control the disease.

Experiments with eradication of the tick proved more frustrating than work with immunization. Francis experimented with strong disinfectants, vegetable oils, and even with electricity. The electrical experiment proved disastrous. A cow was led into the dipping vat and a charge of electricity applied. The cow dropped dead and the irritated ticks went off to find a new host.

The impact of Francis' work on the nation's cattle industry was great; the impact of his work on the Texas cattle industry was greater still. Texas could now begin to develop quality beef herds by importing new breed stock. Francis' successes marked the beginning of the modern Texas cattle industry. He fully deserved the epithet "father of the Texas cattle industry."

Efforts to control Texas fever not only provided the broad impetus behind the establishment of A&M's

Dr. Mark Francis lectures to an early group of veterinary students. Courtesy Texas A&M University Archives.

School of Veterinary Medicine, but gave a very direct and immediate impulse to Governor Ferguson's support for such a school. Texas fever was only the beginning of a long string of veterinary victories. In the decades after 1900, veterinarians at College Station worked extensively and with considerable success in treating or preventing anthrax, black leg, tetanus, rabies, and, especially, hog-cholera.

On April 16, 1916, the board of directors established the School of Veterinary Medicine as a part of the Agricultural and Mechanical College. The school was authorized to award the degree of Doctor of Veterinary Medicine. Dr. Mark Francis was named dean and professor of veterinary medicine and surgery.

By 1918, even the new facilities appeared inadequate. The school converted the old wooden bath houses into a dissecting room. In 1933, a veterinary anatomy building and several stables were constructed. By 1955, the new, modern veterinary hospital, office, and laboratory building was completed.

In 1913, another man who was to play an important role in the history of the A&M College of Veterinary Medicine joined the faculty. Dr. Hubert Schmidt was named assistant to Mark Francis at the Texas Agricultural Experiment Station. Schmidt first worked with Francis on Texas fever and later made important studies of animal diseases caused by mineral deficiencies. Partly through his work, proper mineral supplements have almost eliminated these once-prevalent stock diseases from Gulf Coast cattle.

Mark Francis was the father of veterinary medicine in Texas. With Francis, Ross Perry Marsteller, Ralph Clark Dunn, and Hubert Schmidt were the founders of Texas A&M's present College of Veterinary Medicine. These four men achieved a remarkable record of medical discoveries and of service to the profession and to the College.

The School of Veterinary Medicine opened at the beginning of the forty-first term of A&M, in September of 1916. Only freshman classes were taught the first year; the second, third, and fourth year classes were added each consecutive year. The four departments of the new school included anatomy, medicine and surgery, pharmacology, and pathology. The curriculum in veterinary medicine was, in fact, a regular four-year college course that included fifteen semester hours of biology, nine hours of chemistry, twenty-one hours of English, six hours of physics, nine hours of animal husbandry, and three hours each of dairy husbandry and entomology. The remaining courses were in veterinary medicine. Students were required

to participate in ROTC and to take twelve hours of military science in the first two years, but were exempt from the ROTC and Corps of Cadets in the junior and senior years.

Anticipating the first graduating class from the School of Veterinary Medicine, the Thirty-sixth Texas Legislature passed an act "Regulating the Practice of Veterinary Medicine, Surgery, and Dentistry, and Creating a Board of Veterinary Medical Examiners."

By 1930, the school was instructing 161 students. Only eighteen of these, however, were enrolled in the regular veterinary medicine course. Most of the students were enrolled in either animal husbandry or poultry science.

Enrollments began to surge during the depression and burgeoned after World War II. By 1936, the school was facing the situation of being severely overpopulated and understaffed. The American Veterinary Association became critical of the school's deficiencies and called upon Texas A&M "to increase the staff and the number of departments commensurate with the education standards and expanding accumulation of knowledge in the field of veterinary medicine."

Admission standards were raised and first applied to the class of 1941. The new standards made veterinary medicine more than a specialized college curriculum. Later, in 1951, two years of preparatory college work became part of the requirement for admission to the veterinary medicine curriculum, further elevating the work into the graduate or professional level. Sixteen new members were added to the veterinary medicine faculty in 1936 and 1937, which more than doubled the existing staff.

Enrollment declined somewhat during the years of World War II, but the postwar surge created new crises for the school and for the entire College.

On September 1, 1948, Dr. Ivan Bertrand Boughton became dean of the School of Veterinary Medicine. He reorganized the school, and veterinary extension and research facilities were incorporated with the academic programs. This reorganization helped the school appear to conform more fully to the standards of the American Veterinary Medicine Association. Dean Boughton suffered a severe stroke in 1952, and in 1953 Dr. Willis W. Armistead was named the new dean. Armistead accepted the position of dean of the Michigan State University Veterinary Medical School in 1957, and Dr. Alvin A. Price was selected to replace him. Price, a firm advocate of the practice of learning by doing, oriented the whole program in veterinary medicine at A&M toward student participation.

Forest conservation has grown from an idea to a science in the years since the foundation of the Forest Service. Courtesy Texas Forest Service.

Fire fighting and fire prevention are important aspects of the Texas Forest Service's overall mission. Courtesy Texas Forest Service.

Under Price's leadership, admission quotas continued to be enforced in order to maintain the quality of the program. By 1963, only sixty-four new students per year were being admitted to the College of Veterinary Medicine. In that year too, Sonja Oliphant became the first woman admitted to veterinary medicine, mating another historic landmark at A&M. In 1973, George C. Shelton was named dean of veterinary medicine, and the college made new efforts to meet the needs of and provide expanded services to the people of Texas.

Responding to the ever-changing demands of society, Texas A&M's College of Veterinary Medicine became the first in the nation to offer a program in the medicine of aquatic animals. The establishment of the Texas Veterinary Medical Diagnostic Laboratory and the Institute of Comparative Medicine further broadened the horizons of service.

Like the College of Veterinary Medicine, the Texas Forest Service has come a long way since its inception. During the twenties and thirties agriculture and agricultural extension people had little interest in, and little concept of, "tree farming." The Forest Service tended to be the stepchild of the College's main effort in agriculture and engineering. The Forest Ser-

vice itself was regarded generally as a nonacademic, forest-firefighting brigade.

Despite its low-key characterization, a role which it continues to occupy within the broad efforts of Texas A&M, the Texas Forest Service has worked quietly and efficiently since 1915 for the improvement and protection of Texas forest resources. Its works, like those of the Texas Agricultural Extension Service, have had a profound impact upon the lives of millions of Texans.

The Texas Forest Service is distinguished from other state agencies by several uncommon characteristics, including the fact that its primary operational activities are largely confined to approximately forty deep-East Texas counties, where most Texas timber production exists. This gives the service a more regional than statewide complexion—a situation not without political and fiscal implications. The unforested regions which comprise most of Texas have necessarily had relatively little empathy for the Forest Service. This situation is rapidly changing, however, for Texans everywhere are coming to understand the value of timber resources, state parks, and recreation areas.

Under the leadership of Chief Forester Gifford Pinchot and President Theodore Roosevelt, the National Forest Service was created by the act of February 1, 1905. Until halted by Congress in 1907, Roosevelt used his executive powers to transfer millions of acres of forest lands and dam sites from the public domain to national forests.

As of 1911, Texas had no public program of forest protection or conservation. Considerable interest in and support for such a forestry program, however, had been developed through the efforts of W. Goodrich Jones, a Temple businessman and banker generally accepted as the "father of Texas forestry." On the instigation of Dr. Bernard Eduard Fernow, chief of the newly created Division of Forestry in the U.S. Department of Agriculture, Jones, in 1898, began a crusade for the creation of a Texas forestry agency. Support became sufficiently strong for Jones to have a forestry bill introduced into the state legislature in 1913. The bill failed to pass.

The Texas Forestry Association, organized in 1914, supported passage of a Texas forestry law, and such a law was passed in 1915. The law was designed to protect forest lands from fire and exploitation and called for the appointment of a state forester by the board of directors of Texas A&M. James H. Foster, professor of forestry at New Hampshire College of Agriculture and Mechanics, was named the first state forester of Texas.

A fire-protection program was begun in 1915, aided somewhat by federal monies. The program encompassed about thirty counties and thirteen million acres of land in East Texas. Six "federal patrolmen" were hired to ride horseback fifteen to twenty-five miles a day to meet the people of the districts, acquaint them with the fire protection program, post public fire notices, distribute literature, and extinguish small fires with the help of local citizens.

Foster published *Bulletin 1* of the Department of Forestry in 1916, which attempted to create concern over "Grass and Woodland Fires in Texas."

One of the most important efforts of the Forest Service during Foster's administration was the compilation of a "General Survey of Texas Woodlands." His sixth forestry bulletin was on the causes of and concern for forest fires in Texas. The report pointed out that soil erosion and depletion, as well as the long-term loss of future forests and game, are products of forest fires.

The primary efforts of the forestry agency in the early days were educational and informational. In terms of actually curbing fire losses, success was mini-

mal. The important aspect of Foster's work, however, was not the degree of protection his patrolmen provided Texas forests, but the development of the idea that those forests even needed protecting.

By 1917, however, Foster had failed to stimulate effectively the Texas legislature. In November of that year, he stated that the service had reached the limits of its capacity. He resigned the next year, apparently convinced that the future of the Forest Service in Texas was bleak.

The board appointed Eric O. Siecke to succeed Foster. Under Siecke's direction, the Texas forestry agency made the transition from stressing an educational and informational role to the status of being an operations-oriented state agency. The State Forestry Agency, or Department of Forestry as it was officially known, was renamed the Texas Forest Service in 1926. Siecke was an energetic and positive leader, who, during his long tenure from 1918 to 1942, expanded the operations and effectiveness of the Forest Service.

Appropriations increased after World War I, and the number of fire patrolmen was raised from nine to twenty-two. A Division of Forest Protection was established. The number of patrolmen continued to increase, until there were forty-two patrolmen and four inspectors by 1926. Fire-control effectiveness demonstrated a marked improvement over the decades of the twenties and thirties, an improvement attributed as much to public education as to practical fire control.

The service increasingly stressed forests as a crop. The first state forest of 1,701 acres was purchased in 1924 in Newton County. In 1925, a second forest was acquired, and more tracts were to follow. Between 1934 and 1937, 631,000 acres were acquired by the federal government.

Public forestry work was expanded tremendously by the Civilian Conservation Corps (CCC) programs operating in conjunction with the Texas Forest Service between 1934 and 1941. The CCC helped modernize the Texas Forest Service and greatly improved fire-protection capabilities.

By 1938, the Texas Forest Service had developed four major divisions: the Divisions of Forest Management, Forest Education, Forest Research, and Forest Protection. William E. White headed the Division of Forest Protection in 1938 and succeeded E. O. Siecke as director of the Texas Forest Service in 1942.

The critical shortage of men during World War II stimulated new innovations and new demands on the

An early forest patrolman, W. E. Wells, traveled on horseback around 1921 to encourage the prevention of forest fires. Courtesy Texas Forest Service.

Paul R. Kramer, director of the Texas Forest Service from *1967* to *1981*. Courtesy Texas Forest Service.

Bruce Miles, director of the Texas Forest Service since *1981*. Courtesy Texas Forest Service.

Texas Forest Service. The Texas Forest Patrol was organized to provide air surveillance of forests during critical fire periods. Increased timber production became the number one war-time commitment of the service. After the war, the housing boom placed a new urgency on fire protection, timber management, and production utilization.

Director White resigned in 1948, and Sherman L. ("Jack") Frost replaced him for a short time. Frost was succeeded by David A. ("Andy") Anderson. In 1949, the board named a permanent director of the Texas Forest Service, Alfred D. Folweiler, who served until 1967.

Changes in College leadership and the high incidence of fires contributed to the Texas lumber industry's lack of faith in the service. Timber prices were soaring. The Texas lumber industry was becoming better organized and more influential. The Texas Lumber Manufacturers Association (TLMA) decided something had to be done to improve the quality of fire-protection services in Texas. Their efforts brought about the appointment of Albert E. Cudlipp, secretary-treasurer of TLMA, to the A&M Board. Cudlipp

succeeded in bringing Board attention to the needs and importance of the Forest Service.

Timber interests believed the Texas Forest Service was being neglected because of A&M's emphasis on agriculture and engineering. There was no interest in separating the service from A&M, but there were efforts to make it a more equal partner in the system.

One of the most important developments of these years was the establishment of an advisory committee to the service. It effectively integrated the service with representatives of the industry it served and helped make it more responsive to owners of forest land and to the forest-products industries.

Folweiler reorganized the field-protection services of the agency. Expanded operations and upgrading of the service required substantial increases in state appropriations. Fortunately, there were concerned men both in and out of the legislature.

Folweiler retired as director in 1967 and was succeeded by Paul R. Kramer. Kramer expanded forestry research and reforestation and management programs. Public education, as well as forest protection, contin-

A fire-fighting crew with two-way radio equipped truck/tractor unit. In the background is one of the two hundred steel towers used by the Texas Forest Service. Courtesy Texas Forest Service.

Aggies replant trees to replace those cut for the annual Bonfire. Courtesy Texas A&M University Photographic Services.

The Forest Genetics Laboratory greenhouse on the Texas A&M campus, where research in tree improvement is conducted. Courtesy Texas Forest Service.

Cutting timber for the Aggie bonfire in *1955*, an "extracurricular" Forest Service job. Left: Larry Kennedy; right: Ernest Biehunko, Ross Volunteers commander. Courtesy Texas A&M University Archives.

The Texas Forest Service performs many duties designed to protect and promote the state's timber resources. Courtesy Texas Forest Service.

The concept of tree farming has grown considerably under the direction of the Forest Service. Courtesy Texas Forest Service.

The Texas Forest Service continually monitors conditions in the state's timber areas. Courtesy Texas Forest Service.

"The Extension Service had humble beginnings, but its great value to farmers was quickly recognized..."

ues to be a major effort of the Texas Forest Service. Research programs have developed new and improved tree-farming practices. Trained foresters have taught timber-land owners the best forestry practices. The Texas Forest Service has performed an invaluable public service in increasing public awareness of the importance of conservation and forest preservation.

Texas A&M established an undergraduate degree program in forestry in 1969. The School of Natural Bio-Science, which complements forestry programs at A&M, was created in 1965.

Throughout their history the forestry programs and the Texas Forest Service have carried a low profile within the state and within the Texas A&M academic system, but in dollars and cents and in public service, the forestry programs and the Texas Forest Service have had a profound impact upon Texas and the nation. The service has strongly adhered to the institution's recognized obligation to serve the people.

Another service that has been of great benefit to the public is the Texas Agricultural Extension Service. Its purpose was clearly stated in the beginning:

Extension work is hereby defined as all work intended to extend the usefulness of the College to the people of the state...

—Texas A&M Board of Directors,
October 15, 1912

Tent headquarters of the Extension Department at Texas A&M, before the Smith-Lever Act created the Cooperative Agricultural Extension Service. Courtesy Texas A&M University Archives.

The passage of the Morrill Land-Grant Act in 1862 marked the real beginning of organized public agricultural extension work in the United States. Teaching, research, and extension developed as coordinate divisions of the land-grant college effort. A&M first conceived of its extension obligations in the 1880s, developed programs in the 1890s, and adopted the format of modern extension work in the first decade of the twentieth century. A Department of Extension was created in 1910, and the College entered into a cooperative agreement with the U.S. Department of Agriculture and formally organized a state-wide extension program in 1912. Texas A&M organized the Texas Agricultural Extension Service under the provisions of the Smith-Lever Act of 1914, which provided for cooperative agricultural extension work between the land-grant colleges and the U.S. Department of Agriculture. Extension, by that time, had already become an established fact in Texas and in many other states.

By 1878, the Texas Grange had become concerned that Texas A&M, by adhering to the classic literary curricula during its early years, was failing in its obligations to the people. A result of this concern was the establishment of an experimental farm. After 1888, the Agricultural Experiment Station conducted studies for improving crops and cultivation techniques.

George Washington Curtis, who joined the faculty as professor of agriculture in 1883, played a large part in the early development of demonstration work. He recommended the establishment of "farmers' institutes" to allow "free discussion and experimentation." He also began the publication of bulletins making available to the public the results of experimental farm work.

With appropriations from the legislature, the first farmer's institute was held in Texas in Henrietta, in 1890, and further meetings followed across the state. The Texas Farmers' Congress was organized in 1898, with James H. Connell as its first president. Connell

W. C. Stallings, first county agent in the United States, and his group of Smith County Corn Club boys (a predecessor of the 4-H Club) pose in a model corn field in 1909. Courtesy Texas A&M University Archives.

Dr. Seaman A. Knapp played a great role in developing Texas' and the nation's Agricultural Experiment Station and Agricultural Extension Service programs. Courtesy Texas A&M University Archives.

replaced Curtis as professor of agriculture and director of the Agricultural Experiment Station. The congress met annually on the A&M campus from 1898 to 1915. It proved a most effective device in bringing the farmer in to see demonstration farm work, to hear lectures, and to obtain practical scientific farming information. It was A&M's first well-organized extension activity.

The Farm Boys' and Girls' Progressive League was organized in 1903. The league was a predecessor of 4-H Club work.

Appointment of Seaman A. Knapp as special agent of the U.S. Department of Agriculture played an important role in developing sound practices in the field and promoting public interest. Knapp helped establish a number of government-operated demonstration farms, gave assistance and direction in solving farm problems in Texas, and aided in creating interest in the establishment of the Porter Demonstration Farm at Terrell, Texas. The Porter farm proved eminently successful. It was not a government farm, nor a corporate farm, but a local, community farm operated at local expense. Knapp also mobilized the industrial agents of Texas railroads to support efforts to combat

the boll weevil and to promote better farming techniques among farmers served by their roads.

Texas A&M officially entered the picture in 1905, when the state legislature failed to make appropriations for the continuance of Farmers' Institute and Farmers' Congress work at A&M. Knapp agreed to help fund the College's program. A&M agreed to take charge of a minimum of twenty demonstration farms. This established an important precedent for A&M's direction of county or demonstration agent work. The demonstration idea rapidly spread across Texas into other states.

Between 1906 and 1911, the extension idea was also being promoted by the General Education Board, a John D. Rockefeller-funded organization, which had concluded a cooperative agreement with the Department of Agriculture in 1906.

In 1910, Texas A&M established correspondence courses in agricultural education for teachers, and in soils, crops, dairying, animal husbandry, and horticulture for farmers. A Department of Extension was also established.

In 1911, the Texas legislature approved a bill that gave the county agent-extension program in Texas a firm base and opened new horizons in extension work.

In *1906,* W. C. Stallings of Smith County, Texas, became the first county agent in the United States appointed to serve only one county. Courtesy Texas A&M University Archives.

Walter C. Porter, on whose farm at Terrell Seaman A. Knapp established the first demonstration farm in Texas in *1902.* Courtesy Texas A&M University Archives.

Every county in Texas now had the ability to hire its own county agent without dependence upon private donations or federal funds. By October, thirteen Texas counties had either converted to the new system of funding county agents or had initiated new programs.

The advent of the Farm Bureau, which began as a sponsoring organization for extension agents, marked yet another chapter in the extension story. New state legislation facilitated the expansion of the extension program and "localized" what otherwise might have been a federal or national program.

In August, 1912, the directors announced a new extension policy for Texas A&M, which broadened the College's role and declared a policy to "achieve distinction for civil service to the people of Texas." A new Extension Committee was formed, defining the role and function of A&M's program; it recommended specific actions, which included expansion of correspondence courses and faculty participation in public and professional affairs.

In 1912, Edna W. Trigg was the first "lady agent" appointed in Texas, and by the end of the year sixteen home demonstration agents were in service. Enrollment in boys' and girls' club work rose to over fifteen thousand. Exhibits, fairs, shows, and demonstrations were held in almost every area of Texas. By 1913, the county agents and agricultural extension had become well-established institutions in the state.

The development of agricultural extension promoted a great awakening at the College and aided a genuine surge of academic progress.

Passage and implementation of the Smith-Lever Act enabled A&M further to broaden its extension efforts. Nine new agricultural specialists were appointed to the extension staff in 1915. For the first time, African-American county and district agents were appointed in the Texas extension program.

By 1927, on the eve of the silver anniversary of the Extension Service, there were about three hundred county and home demonstration agents in the

Mrs. Edna W. Trigg was the first home demonstration agent in Texas. Courtesy Texas A&M University Archives.

The Jack County, Texas, Boys' Corn Club is claimed to be the first 4-H Club in the United States. Courtesy Texas A&M University Archives.

The *Agricultural Extension Service staff and its director, Thomas O. Walton (directly in front of the woman in the upper left), about 1924. Courtesy Texas A&M University Archives.*

Texas Agricultural Extension agents at a 4-H convention in Waco in 1912. Courtesy Texas A&M University Archives.

Emus—something new in Texas Agribusiness—are checked at the
Veterinary Medical School. Photograph by Michael Kellett. Courtesy
Texas A&M University Photographic Services.

One of the College of Veterinary Medicine's unique features—guide dog
service. Photograph by Michael Kellett. Courtesy Texas A&M University
Photographic Services.

field and forty-eight staff members at College Station.

By 1935, extension services had grown to gigantic proportions. The Capper-Ketcham Act of 1928 had provided large new federal appropriations to the states, and the Agricultural Adjustment Act of 1933 had further aided growth. The Bankhead-Jones Act of 1935 provided additional money for both Texas A&M's Agricultural Experiment Station and the Extension Service. Howard H. Williamson succeeded Oscar Baker Martin as director on July 8, 1935.

World War II brought tremendous external and internal pressures to bear upon the College and the Texas Extension Service. As in World War I, the Extension Service had a job to do—to promote agricultural production. Also, there was a big turnover in personnel, especially among the younger men entering and returning from military service. In addition, there were tremendous technological breakthroughs and developments in every area of science and technology—and in agriculture. By 1943, these developments and pressures of growth and change combined to create a crisis in the Texas Agricultural Extension Service. Texas A&M needed to change with the times. Top personnel were realigned. Programs were reappraised. The Extension Service was placed under the auspices of the newly created vice president for agriculture, David Willard Williams, and reorganization measures were effected.

A more fundamental reorganization also occurred in 1946, when the academic divisions of the School of Agriculture were integrated to include personnel from the School of Agriculture, the Texas Agricultural Experiment Station, and the Agricultural Extension Service. This reorganization was in line with A&M's goals of coordinating teaching, research, and extension activities.

Directors Ide Peebles Trotter (1944–49) and George G. Gibson (1949–58) streamlined and expanded the role of extension work on the farm and in rural and urban communities.

John E. Hutchison, who became director of the Texas Extension Service in 1958, believed that the role and scope of the modern cooperative extension service had broadened to meet the developing needs of an urban society. Under his direction, the agency is no longer exclusively farm- and rural-oriented. The program now includes such services as continuing educational programs for elected and nonelected officials of county government, special programs for the aging, and programs in mental health and mental retardation. Extension provides a "sophisticated system of informal education" designed to meet the changing needs of modern society, in almost every area of human endeavor.

The Texas Engineering Extension Service offers technical information and assistance to Texas engineers, industry, and business. It complements the testing and research services of the Texas Engineering Experiment Station and the Texas Transportation Institute. The Cyclotron Institute, the Center for Tectonophysics, and centers or programs for Business and Economic Analysis, Chemical Characterization and Analysis, Drug Prevention and Education, Energy and Mineral Resources, Housing and Urban Development, International Business Studies, Executive Development, and Private Enterprise Research (to mention only a few), broaden the role and scope of the university to serve a very diverse and distant public.

*"I was probably the first Aggie to receive seven letters—
three in football, one in baseball, one in track,
one in hell raising, and one from the faculty
telling me they didn't need me anymore ..."*

C. W. Taylor (left) was the first paid football coach at A&M. Others pictured here in *1898* are top,
left to right: Johnson, Love, R. B. Bocttcher; bottom: Taylor, Hal Moseley, Dornell, Astin, and Tracy. Courtesy Texas A&M University Archives.

VII.

Gig 'em Aggies

Modern, organized sports, particularly football and baseball, began at Texas A&M in the 1890s. The "dark ages" of athletics at A&M lasted until about 1915, when the organization of the Southwest Conference invigorated the entire athletic program at Texas A&M and throughout the state and region. Even before this, by 1910, Texas A&M Aggies had already gone "hog-wild" over football. At the end of World War I, big-time intercollegiate athletics were here to stay.

Thirty-five thousand people, for example, jammed the new football stadium at Austin on Thanksgiving Day in 1924 to witness what had already become a regional if not a national classic—the annual football game between Texas A&M and the University of Texas. Commented one unenthusiastic reporter of the event: "The country is simply going hog-wild over football. America is essentially a nation of sports, and we would not deny them a reasonable pastime in this regard, but Americans are extremists, just the same."

Football began on the A&M campus in the fall of 1892. By February of the next year, cadets claimed that "A&MC now boasts a crack football team." In 1894, the "Farmers" defeated Ball High School in Galveston, 14-6. That same year, in the first game with the University of Texas, they lost by a disastrous 38-0. The A&M "Farmers" defeated Austin College 22-0, downed Houston High School 28-0, and tied Ball High School

0-0 in 1896. In that year A&M students adopted their first official yell:

> Rah! Rah! Rah!
> Hi! Ho! Ha!
> AMC
> Boom! Cis! Bah!
> College!

The Aggies were a rough-tough, hell-raising bunch, according to Josh B. Sterns, one of the pioneers of Texas A&M football. Sterns recalled many years later that he was "probably the first Aggie to receive seven letters—three in football, one in baseball, one in track, one in hell raising and one from the faculty telling me they didn't need me anymore."

In 1897, the boys hired their own coach, C. W. Taylor. The hat was passed for Taylor at football games, to pay his salary.

In 1897, the Aggies lost to Houston High School 10-0. They were defeated by TCU 30-6. They beat Austin College 4-0.

In 1899, the "Cadets" lost to the University of Texas 6-0. The referees ruled an A&M touchdown illegal, and the *Battalion* announced that the Aggies were robbed:

> Our players proved that they have grit,
> And played an honest game,

A&M beats LSU 52-0, on December 2, 1899. Courtesy Texas A&M University Archives.

W. A. Murray, A&M's third football coach, 1899. Courtesy Texas A&M University Archives.

The 1900 Aggie football team poses for an official portrait. Faculty representative B. C. Pittuck wears the black hat on the left, Coach W. A. Murray the white hat on the right. Players are front, left to right: Gray, Moseley, Hyde, unidentified, Davidson, McGinnis, Shultz, Carpenter; rear: Davenport, Erhardt, Roble, Thrower, James, Brown, Foster, unidentified, Williams, Jordan. Courtesy Texas A&M University Archives.

Games were played in front of Old Main until the board of directors set aside an athletic field in *1906* on the location of what is now Kyle Field. Courtesy Texas A&M University Archives.

Texas Aggie football captain Reaville M. Brown, *1900*. Courtesy Texas A&M University Archives.

Coach Charles B. Moran, who joined the A&M staff in *1909*, compiled a staggering record of successes. Courtesy Texas A&M University Archives.

> The referee robbed them 6 to 0
> They held Varsity just the same.

A&M played the University of Texas in football every year, and often twice a year, from 1898 through 1911. The *Dallas News* reported the 1902 upset victory:

> For the first time in the history of the game in Texas the State University team went down in defeat before the State Agricultural and Mechanical College eleven and it was the first time that team has ever scored against the varsity. The College boys and their friends are painting the town red tonight, while everything is silent and dark on the local campus.

The A&M faculty did not share the cadets's enthusiasm for football. Prior to 1902, they had passed a ruling prohibiting the A&M team from meeting other institutions in competitive events. A vigorous student protest caused the faculty to rescind their action.

Texas A&M's Directors called for the creation of a permanent student-faculty committee to supervise athletic events. Texas A&M's General Athletic Associa-

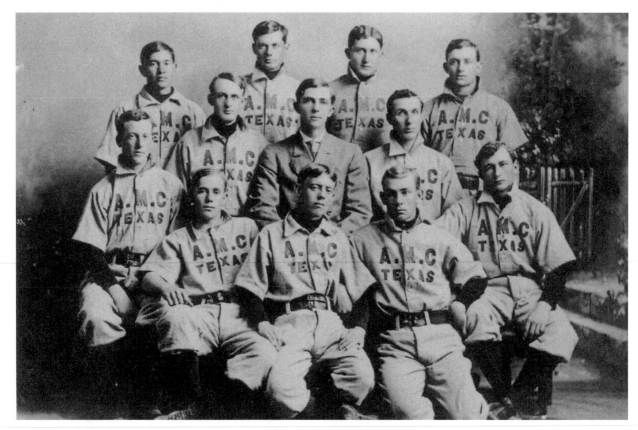

The Aggie baseball team, about 1908. Courtesy Texas A&M University Archives.

Members of the 1908 Campus Tennis Club. Courtesy Texas A&M University Archives.

Kyle Field, about 1910. Courtesy Texas A&M University Archives.

tion, which in 1906 was renamed the Athletic Council, was established to recommend coaches, schedule games, award letters, and conduct athletic business policy.

College athletics were regularized by the organization in Waco, Texas, of the Southwestern Inter-Collegiate Athletics Association on March 12, 1904. This association, forerunner of the Southwest Conference, included, in the beginning, Baylor University, Southwestern University, Trinity University, the University of Texas, and Texas A&M. They were soon joined by Austin College, Fort Worth University, Missouri School of Mines, the University of Oklahoma, and Washington University.

Texas A&M's award to lettermen was changed from a C for College, to a T for Texas. The T Association, with membership open to all students and former students who had represented A&M in intercollegiate athletics, was organized in 1907. The T was awarded until 1915, when it was overlaid with the AMC to distinguish the A&M T from the University of Texas T.

Most of the early games were played on the drill field at A&M, where spectators simply stood or sat in carriages around the field. Some games were played in Bryan at the fair grounds, which boasted a grandstand. In 1904, the board set aside an area on the campus as a permanent athletic field. At that time, Edwin Jackson Kyle, who joined the faculty as professor of horticulture, was chairman of the Athletic Council. Kyle first had the area fenced off with barbed wire, then replaced the wire with a wooden fence. In addition, the covered grandstand at Bryan's fair grounds was purchased. Kyle gave a personal note since the council had no money. The five-hundred seat stadium was moved and rebuilt on campus during the 1906 season.

The field soon became known as Kyle Field. There was some controversy, later, regarding whether the field was named for Edwin Jackson Kyle or Dr. J. Allen Kyle, a member of the board. The board has decreed that it was indeed named for Edwin Jackson Kyle, who was without question a great inspiration and tireless worker in the development of A&M's athletic program.

Sports reached a high point at College Station in 1908. Still, in that year, the "Farmers" completed their first losing season in six years with a 3-5-0 record. One of the losses, to the University of Texas, was particularly onerous. At one point, the Longhorns led 14-0. Enthusiastic Longhorn supporters conducted an impromptu victory ceremony by rushing onto the field with brooms and figuratively sweeping the Aggies

The *1910* football team, coached by Charles B. Moran. Standing left to right: Coach Moran, Manager Walter Scott Moore; third row: *White, Bateman, Beasley, Flinchum, Hohn, Grisson, Cratcher*; middle: *Lambert, unidentified, Abbott, Bell, Altgelt*; front: *Ward, Schaudel, Barnes, Kern, McDowell*. Courtesy Texas A&M University Archives.

During his six seasons at A&M, Charles B. Moran's teams won *38* games, lost *8*, and tied *4*, compiling *1,091* points against the opponents' 190. At the Thanksgiving Day game in *1949*, Frank C. Bolton (left) and Caesar Hohn, one of Moran's great players, dedicated a plaque to Coach Moran. Courtesy Texas A&M University Archives.

Aggie baseballers, about *1910–11*. Courtesy Texas A&M University Archives.

Aggies branded the UT mascot with the score of the *1915* game. Alterations to the brand resulted in the word which became the name of the UT mascot—BEVO. *Courtesy Texas A&M University Archives.*

The Southwest Conference organized in *1915.* Here, in *1917,* a group of sophomores help the team get Rice's goat. Final score of the game, A&M *10,* Rice *0. Courtesy Texas A&M University Archives.*

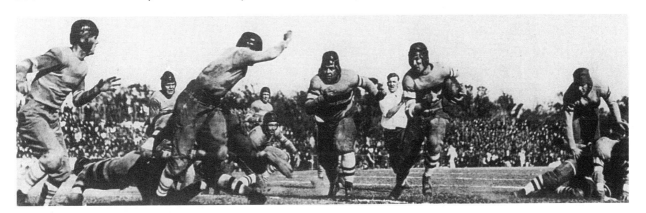

Football, 1917—one of eight games in which A&M was not scored upon. Total season score: 270-0! *Courtesy Texas A&M University Archives.*

In eleven seasons at Texas A&M, between *1917* and *1928,* Dana X. Bible's teams won the Southwest Conference five times. *Courtesy Texas A&M University Archives.*

from the field. The cadets were infuriated. They poured onto the field to join the fray. General riot reigned in the stadium. Many A&M and University of Texas students were bruised. Clothing was torn and hats smashed. Relations between the A&M and the University student bodies, already strained, were considerably soured.

Coach Ned A. Merriam was replaced in 1909 by Charles B. Moran, who said he "came here to win." Indeed he did. He compiled thirty-eight wins, eight losses, and four ties in six football seasons. He acquired the reputation of being a tough, mean fighter. It was thought, on occasion, that he used professional ball players in his line-up, and certainly he imported some fine talent from places such as the Haskell (Indian) Institute in Oklahoma. His 1912 team, with 366 points to 26 against nine opponents, still holds the season scoring record for the Aggies. His team included the immortals Caesar ("Dutch") Hohn and Tyree Bell, among others.

E. King Gill, the original "Twelfth Man." Courtesy Texas A&M University Archives.

R. H. ("Chick") Harrison, Jr., A&M football letterman in 1918 and 1919. Courtesy Texas A&M University Archives.

Basketball made its first appearance at A&M in 1913. That year A&M beat Marlin High School 78-8 and Galveston YMCA 72-14 (and lost to that team in a second match 25-27). That same year A&M downed Sam Houston Normal Institute 72-9 in one match and 40-12 in the second, and closed the season with a 26-24 loss to Houston High School. Enthusiasm for basketball was slow to build, but the game gradually gained footing as a regular college sport.

Track and baseball were the first organized sports on the campus. Texas A&M played its first baseball game against Navasota in 1891. The contest erupted into a rhubarb, and the game was finally awarded to A&M by a score of 9-4. Football took over in popularity in 1893, and baseball declined. Wirt Spencer, the first regular baseball coach, guided the team from 1904 until 1908 and compiled twenty-nine wins, twenty-eight losses, and three ties. Moran, who coached the team through 1914, compiled fifty wins, forty-six losses, and five ties.

A&M held its first invitational track meet in 1899. In 1910, the Aggies fielded a great track team that won the first annual meet of the Texas Intercollegiate Athletic Association. William A. McDonald broke the record in the 120-yard hurdles. Roger Hooker tied the record in the 16-pound shotput.

Organized athletics truly came of age with the establishment of the Southwest Conference in 1914. Texas A&M, Baylor, Rice Institute, Oklahoma A&M, Southwestern University, and the Universities of Arkansas, Texas, and Oklahoma agreed to a compact creating the conference. The composition of the Southwest Conference has changed considerably since that time. New teams have joined and others have withdrawn, but that initial gathering was the "kickoff" for organized athletics in the southwest.

Moran resigned in 1914, and A&M reorganized its program under an athletic director, William L. Driver, formerly coach at the University of Mississippi. E. H. W. ("Jigger") Harlan of Princeton became

Aggie baseball, about *1920*—Higgie covering third. Roswell G. Higginbotham was a *1973* A&M Athletic Hall of Fame honoree. Courtesy Texas A&M University Archives.

"Slide!" Aggie baseball about *1920*. Courtesy Texas A&M University Archives.

head coach in football. Dana X. Bible came to A&M in 1915 as freshman coach, left in 1916, and returned to become head coach for the 1917 season. Beginning with that season, when the Aggies went undefeated and unscored on, Bible began to compile one of the most remarkable coaching records of all time.

Pole vaulting, *1920*. Courtesy Texas A&M University Archives.

In both 1918 and 1919, his Aggie teams were undefeated. Not a single point was scored against A&M in 1919. The 1919 Thanksgiving Day game between A&M and the University of Texas marked two firsts in football history. Probably the first play-by-play radio broadcast of the game took place via ham radio station 5YA, located in the Electrical Engineering Building. That game also marked the first annual Thanksgiving contest between A&M and the University of Texas.

The winning season of 1919 produced enthusiastic support among former students and football fans for the College's athletic program. The council began to search for ways to build a stadium. A fund drive foundered, and it was 1927 before the College decided to build a stadium with funds derived from the sale of revenue bonds.

Meanwhile, Bible's team continued to compile outstanding records. In 1920, the Aggies won 6, tied 1, and lost to Texas by a score of 7-3. Next year's record was 6-1-2. The Aggies played in one of the first postseason bowl games on record, the Dixie Classic, at Fair Park Stadium in Dallas, January 2, 1922. Centre College's "Praying Colonels" were undefeated and unscored on throughout 1921. They had beaten such teams as Clemson, Harvard, Kentucky, and Auburn. A&M beat the Kentucky eleven by 22-14. The Texas Aggies were dubbed the "Southern Champions."

The 1922 Centre game will be remembered for another reason. During the game, E. King Gill, a 165-pound reserve sophomore fullback, was in the press box serving as a spotter. As the rough game wore on and injuries took their toll, the Aggies were down to only one backfield substitute. Bible called Gill to the playing field and asked him to suit up. Gill donned

The *A&M basketball team, Southwestern champs, 1920.* Left to right: *W. L. Driver (coach), H. L. Burkes, G. B. Gouger, H. N. Glezen, W. H. Williams, H. E. DeLee, J. A. Pierce, G. H. Hartung, E. E. McQuillen (captain), T. A. Dwyer, A. L. Forbes, J. R. Ehlert, L. S. Keen. Courtesy Texas A&M University Archives.*

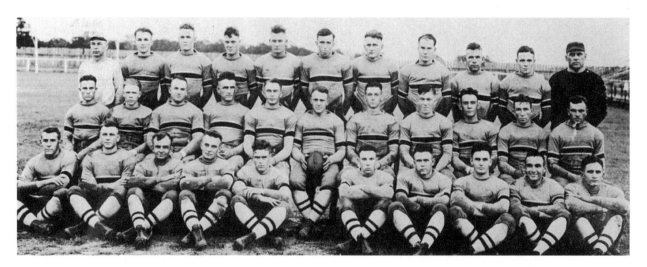

Coach Dana X. Bible (top row, left) and the *1920–21* football team. Front, left to right: *Dieterich, McMillan, Scoffield, Weir, Morris, Smith, Buckner, Frazier, Ballard, Winn;* middle: *Sanders, Gouger, Murrah, Drake, Higginbotham, Mahan, Martin, Scudder, Beasley, Pierce, Wendt;* rear: *Bible (coach), McClellan, Carruthers, Anglin, Crawford, Wilson, Brown, Ramsey, Swanner, Riggs, Rothgeb (coach). Courtesy Texas A&M University Archives.*

The *Aggie* basketball team, *1928–29*. Rear, left to right: C. F. Bassett (coach), J. D. Harris, R. J. Blount, T. G. Caudle, Joe Brown, C. D. Kauffman, E. K. Martin; middle: W. E. Davis, Noah Webster, S. J. Petty, Harry Keeton, R. C. Bell, C. T. Hoke; front: R. T. Lamb, U. L. Pompell, Johnnie Konecny. Courtesy Texas A&M University Archives.

D. C. ("Spike") Arnold played football at A&M from *1924* to *1926*. Courtesy Texas A&M University Archives.

R. H. ("Bob") Berry served as Aggie quarterback during *1923, 1924,* and *1925*. Courtesy Texas A&M University Archives.

Madison ("Matty") Bell headed the A&M coaching staff from *1929* to *1933*. Courtesy Texas A&M University Archives.

Letterman quarterback W. B. ("Dub") Williams, in *1932*. Courtesy Texas A&M University Archives.

Members of the *Aggie* pitching staff, about *1930*. Left to right: Roswell Higginbotham (coach), Pete Wendt (captain), Tommie Mills, Joe E. Brown, Leland Hunter, C. M. Lagow, Eddie Gorman, A. K. Hawes. Courtesy Texas A&M University Archives.

Basketball letterman Joe Merka, 1933. Courtesy Texas A&M University Archives.

injured Aggie captain Heinie Weir's uniform. He did not play in the game, but legend says his readiness spurred the Aggies to the upset 22-14 victory. Since that experience, Aggie coaches have called upon the fabled "Twelfth Man" on several occasions, and the Corps soon adopted the custom, now a hallowed tradition, of standing for all football games, signifying their readiness to be the Twelfth Man.

During Bible's eleven seasons, the Aggies compiled a record of seventy-two wins, nineteen losses, and nine ties. A&M won five Southwest Conference championships during those years. Two of Bible's teams were unbeaten, untied, and unscored on. He left A&M to become head coach at the University of Nebraska, where he remained from 1929 to 1936, and in 1937, he became head coach at the University of Texas. He retired in 1956, after fifty years in football, one of the all-time truly great coaches.

Football and competitive school spirit reached an intense degree during the 1920s. A riot took place at the 1926 Baylor-A&M game, in which Cadet Charles M. Sessums was killed. Angry cadets decided to march on Baylor, with their cannon in tow, and level it to the ground. They were finally dissuaded from their plot. Athletic relations between A&M and Baylor were suspended until 1931.

Another consequence of the 1920s football spirit was the institution of a new Aggie tradition, the bonfire, which is burned in preparation for the game against the University of Texas. In the fall months when the games were usually played, students, letting off steam before the coming event, welcomed a warm fire to crowd around. Gradually, the pre-Texas-game bonfire became a custom, then a tradition.

Early bonfires were made of community trash, limbs, boxes, and debris. Favorite materials were untended, unwatched, and—one hoped—unoccupied outhouses.

By 1935, students were outdoing themselves in acquiring bonfire materials. On the morning following the 1935 bonfire, Frank G. Anderson, then the newly appointed commandant, reported, "a very irate farmer came to my offices to say the boys had carried off his log barn, lock, stock and barrel." Because of that experience, bonfire building was placed under the control of the commandant, who regulated collection of materials.

The bonfire tradition emerged bigger and better after World War II. The first center pole made exclusively of logs was raised for the 1946 fire, and in 1947 two logs were strapped together to create the first high center pole.

Yell practice, another early custom that has become ritualized over the years, is a time and place where enthusiasm is generated. During football season it is held immediately after supper to enliven the student body for the game on Saturday. The band plays, and yells fill the night.

Madison Bell inherited Bible's job as athletic director and football coach in 1929. Bell encountered rough sledding in 1929. It got rougher in 1930: the Aggies won only two of nine games. Things picked up the next year, with seven wins out of ten games, and the Aggies placed third in the Southwest Conference. After that it was mostly downhill again, and, although a good 6-3-1 record was earned in 1933, Madison Bell's days were numbered. Homer Norton of Centenary College in Shreveport, Louisiana, was hired to replace Bell before the season was even over. Bell went to Southern Methodist University as assistant coach, became head coach, and carried his team to the Rose Bowl in 1935, the year his Mustangs defeated Texas A&M 24-0.

Norton had a few bad years. In 1934, the Aggies won two, lost seven, and tied one. In 1935, it was three wins, seven losses. The next year was better—eight wins, three losses, and one tie. Norton produced three

Homer Norton followed Madison Bell in *1933* and over the next fourteen years led the Aggies to three Southwest Conference championships, a national championship, and four bowl games. Courtesy Texas A&M University Archives.

An Aggie great—"Jarrin'" John Kimbrough, All America, *1939*. Courtesy Texas A&M University Archives.

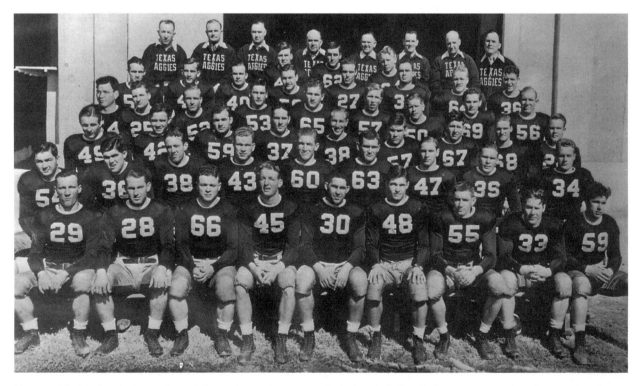

The *1939* undefeated Southwest Conference and National Championship team. Front row: Herbie Smith, Marland Jeffrey, Ed Robnett, Cotton Price, Dookie Pugh, Fim Wood, Jitterbug Henderson, Les Richardson, Joe Rothe; second row: Mack Browder, Muley White, Charley Henke, Marshall Robnett, Tommie Vaughn, Poppa Wesson, Jim Thomason, John Kimbrough, Bud Force, Bama Smith; third row: Cul Rogers, Bill Conatser, Derace Moser, Butch Hermann, Bill Miller, Hugh Boyd, Bill Buchanan, Jim Sterling, Cotton Williams, Bubba Reeves, Martin Ruby; fourth row: Ernie Pannell, Marshall Spivey, Bill Duncan, John Abbott, Zolus Motley, Bill Blessing, Leon Rahn, Harold Cowley, Dog Dawson, Rock Audish; fifth row: Leonard Joeris, Joe Parish, Howard Shelton, Jo-Jo White, Jack Kimbrough, Chip Routt, Carl Geer, Chester Heinmann, Joe Boyd, Gus Bates, Willard Clark; sixth row: Roy Bucek, Henry Hauser, Pinkey Williams; back row: Coaches Marty Karow, Uncle Bill James, Hub McQuillan, Homer Norton, Lil Dimmit, Manning Smith, Harry Faulkner, and Dough Rollins. Courtesy Texas A&M University Archives.

"Bruisin'" Bob Smith receives the Lipscomb-Colson Award as most valuable player on the 1950 team. The award was presented by "Flop" Colson, one of the donors. Courtesy Texas A&M University Archives.

Paul ("Bear") Bryant carried the Aggies to a Southwest Conference victory in 1956, and Gene Stallings led them to a second victory in 1967. Courtesy Texas A&M University Archives.

outstanding players in his 1936 team: Joe Routt, who made All-American and All-Southwest Conference at guard; Charles DeWare, All-Southwest center; and Roy Young, All-Southwest tackle. In 1937, Routt and Young repeated their honors. Dick Todd, a brilliant halfback, and Virgil Jones, a great guard, both made All-Southwest Conference, but the Aggies ended the 1937 season with a 5-2-2 record.

Norton was in trouble. The 1938 season ended with a 4-4-1 record. It was decided to stand pat with Norton for two more years, to run out his contract. Impatient Aggie fans were well advised in this decision—the Aggies won eleven games in 1939, including A&M's only National Championship, the Southwest Conference, and the Sugar Bowl. In that first annual Sugar Bowl contest, A&M defeated Tulane 14-13. Joe Boyd, John Kimbrough, Marshall Robnett, Herb Smith, and Jim Thomason made the All-Southwest Conference team. Boyd and Kimbrough were also named All-Americans. The Aggies defeated Texas 20-0 that season.

Norton did it again next year, taking nine out of ten games. Texas A&M won the conference again in 1941. After the war years, Norton's eleven ended the 1946 season with a 4 win-6 loss record. In 1947, it was 3-6-1. After 1941, A&M won the Southwest Conference in 1956 under Paul ("Bear") Bryant and in 1967 under Gene Stallings.

Football fever, however, never diminished. Robert H. ("Harry") Stiteler, Sr., replaced Norton. The Aggies won no games in 1948 and one in 1949, but they came through with seven wins in 1950. Raymond George took over coaching duties but achieved little better results. In 1954, the Aggies hired Bear Bryant, a proved coach of national reputation. His Aggie team won the Southwest Conference in 1956, defeating Texas by a score of 34-21 in Austin's Memorial Stadium.

Jim Myers and Henry C. ("Hank") Foldberg both coached consecutive losing seasons, from 1958 through 1964. Gene Stallings, a former Aggie player and protégé of Bear Bryant, took over in 1965 and led the Aggies to a 1967 Southwest Conference championship and the Cotton Bowl victory over Bear Bryant's Alabama team, 20-16. But Stallings ended his coaching career at A&M with a final record of 22-39-1. Still seeking the winning combination, the Aggies obtained Emory Bellard from the University of Texas football staff in 1972, to try their luck with the new wishbone formation.

Bellard's bunch fought a tough fight in the 1972

Floor play by the *1949–50* basketball team. Left to right: Wally Moon, John DeWitt, Walt ("Buddy") Davis, Bill Turnbow, Jewell McDowell. Courtesy Texas A&M University Archives.

Gene Stallings coached the Aggies between *1965* and *1971* and brought a Southwest Conference championship to A&M in *1967* and a Cotton Bowl victory over Alabama. Courtesy Texas A&M University Archives.

The *1956* Southwest Conference champions. Front row, left to right: Bobby Lockett, George Gillar, Dennis Goehring, Jack Pardee, Eugene Stallings, Lloyd Hale, Dee Powell, Bob Clendennon, Bobby Keith, Don Watson; second row: Gary Rollins, (manager), John Tracey, John Gilbert, Bill Appelt, Loyd Taylor, Bobby Marks, Roddy Osborne, Murry Trimble, Carl Luna, Allen Goehring, Carlos Esquivel, Joe Schmid (manager); third row: Jim Stanley, Jimmy Wright, John Crow, A. L. Simmons, Ken Beck, Jim Langston, Don Smith, Charles Krueger, Dick Goff, Dick Steadman, Tommy Howard; back row: Richard Gay, Luther Hall, Bobby Conrad, Henry Pearson, Ray Doucet, Leo Wotipka, Don McCelland, Ed Dudley, Lloyd Wasserman, John Polk, Stan Roper. Courtesy Texas A&M University Archives.

Emory Bellard came to A&M in 1972 as athletic director and head coach.
Courtesy Texas A&M University Archives.

season and laid the groundwork for the turn-around in 1973. In that year the Aggies marked up a 5-6 record. The next year, 1974, the Aggies narrowly missed the Southwest Conference championship, being squeezed out by the Baylor Bears, whom the Aggies had defeated in conference play. It was the first trip for the Bears to the Cotton Bowl. A&M and Texas tied for second in conference play. Emory Bellard, like Charles Moran, had "come to win."

Basketball, track, and baseball have continued to thrive, but as minor attractions. Recently, however, these sports have experienced rejuvenation and have assumed the status of major events. Texas A&M has won the Southwest Conference basketball crown on eight occasions. In 1964 and 1969, A&M went to the NCAA playoffs. They tied for Southwest Conference honors in 1951. In 1975, Shelby Metcalf became the only active Southwest Conference basketball coach to chalk up 100 wins. The A&M varsity team turned on the steam in 1975 to give the Aggies one of their best all-time seasons, capturing the conference championship along the way.

Bellard's bunch won an unusual Southwest Conference "tri-championship" in 1975, tieing with the Arkansas Razorbacks and the Texas Longhorns. The Aggies won an invitation to the Liberty Bowl but failed to score against a powerful University of Southern California team. The next year the Aggies finished third in the conference, and beat Florida in the Sun Bowl, 37-14. The Aggies went to the Bluebonnet Bowl in 1977, but in the following year Bellard's famous wishbone offense turned out to be wishful thinking. Emory Bellard resigned mid-season and his offensive coordinator, Tom Wilson, replaced him as head coach. Wilson's Aggies chalked up a 6-5 season for 1979, 4-7 in 1980, and 7-5 in 1981, when they went to the Independence Bowl. Jackie Sherrill replaced Wilson in 1982, and after losing seasons in 1982, 1983, and 1984, he led the Aggies to three consecutive Southwestern Conference championships and Cotton Bowl appearances. Sherrill closed his Texas Aggie career in 1988 with second place in the Southwest Conference and a 6-1-0 record.

When Jackie Sherrill departed, John David Crow, Texas A&M's 1957 Heisman Trophy winner who had been serving under Sherrill as associate athletic director, moved into the director's slot and later, in 1993, became director of athletic development. Wally Groff, with twenty-nine years of experience as business manager and interim athletic director (1981–82) became director of athletics replacing Crow.

R. C. Slocum, with sixteen years of service as an assistant coach at Texas A&M before becoming head coach in 1988, took the Aggies to the John Hancock Bowl and the Holiday Bowl, winning three consecutive Southwest Conference championships in 1991, 1992, and 1993. He accumulated a record as the "winningest" coach in Southwest Conference history. In 1993, the Aggies and the Southwest Conference reached a historic point. Texas A&M, the University of Texas, Texas Tech University, and Baylor University began the process that would take them out of the Southwest Conference and into the Big Eight, reconfiguring that conference into the Big Twelve. Scheduled to begin play in 1996, the new conference includes the four Texas teams with the University of Oklahoma, Oklahoma State University, University of Kansas, Kansas State University, the University of Missouri, the University of Colorado, Iowa State University, and the University of Nebraska.

THE BIG TWELVE CONFERENCE

University	Location	Nickname	Founded	Distance*
Baylor	Waco, TX	Bears	1845	90 miles
Colorado	Boulder, CO	Buffaloes	1876	938 miles
Iowa State	Ames, IA	Cyclones	1868	1,082 miles
Kansas	Lawrence, KN	Jayhawks	1866	695 miles
Kansas State	Manhattan, KN	Wildcats	1863	600 miles
Missouri	Columbia, MO	Tigers	1839	864 miles
Nebraska	Lincoln, NB	Cornhuskers	1869	823 miles
Oklahoma	Norman, OK	Sooners	1890	360 miles
Oklahoma State	Stillwater, OK	Cowboys	1890	445 miles
Texas	Austin, TX	Longhorns	1883	101 miles
Texas A&M	College Station	Aggies	1876	———
Texas Tech	Lubbock, TX	Red Raiders	1923	421 miles

*mileage from College Station, Texas

The Aggie hoopsters repeated in 1975 for another Southwest Conference victory and an overall 21-6 winning season. The Aggies slumped the next two seasons, finishing fourth and seventh, but in the 1978–79 season Metcalf's squad rose to 24-9, defeating Indiana University 54-49 in the Great Alaska Shootout and winning the title in the Golden Gate Invitational in San Francisco. The Aggies then moved to the National Invitational Tournament (NIT), where they defeated New Mexico, 79-68, and Nevada-Reno, 67-64, before losing to Alabama, 72-68.

The next season, 1979–80, was remembered as the best in A&M basketball history to that date. Aggies chalked up a 26-8 season, the Southwest Conference championship, and two NCAA tournament wins, before losing in the final rounds of tournament play. The Aggies slipped to a conference tie for fourth place in 1981, went to the NIT in 1982, and finished third in the conference in 1983 and fifth in 1984. The team tied for second in 1984–85 and tied for the conference championship in 1985–86, accepting a bid to the NIT in both years. Despite overall winning seasons for the next four years, Shelby Metcalf resigned in the middle of the 1989–90 season. John Thornton completed the season, and Kermit Davis, Jr., suffered one of the worst seasons in 1990–91.

Anthony (Tony) Barone, a Duke University graduate, came to A&M as head basketball coach in 1991. The Aggies finished with an even worse record than in the previous year, but a new foundation was laid for better days. Barone's netters moved up to sixth in 1992–93, then tied for second in 1993–94, and that year the team was back on the line for the NIT tournament. The remarkable turnaround of the team from "oblivion to contention" earned Barone selection as the Southwest Conference Coach of the Year, recognition by the United States Basketball Writers Association as the District VI Coach of the Year, and selection by the Texas Association of Basketball Coaches as Texas Senior College Coach of the Year. In February, 1994, Texas A&M University, with Baylor, Texas, and Texas Tech, joined the Big Eight Conference and faced a new and formidable conference alignment for the opening basketball season in 1996, including Kansas, Kansas State, Missouri, Nebraska, Oklahoma, Oklahoma State, Colorado, and Iowa State. Aggie basketball had changed in a big way.

The Aggie baseball team has taken the Southwest Conference championship on twelve occasions since 1915 and has tied for the crown three times. Tom Chandler, A&M's baseball coach for twenty-six years (1958–84), won or shared five conference championships and took the team to the NCAA playoffs on five occasions. During his coaching tenure, sixteen Aggies were named to the baseball All-Americas teams. In 1978, TAMU dedicated its new baseball field to C. E. "Pat" Olsen, a 1923 graduate, and a member of the legendary New York Yankees team that fielded such immortals as Babe Ruth and Lou Gehrig.

When Tom Chandler retired at the close of the 1984 season, Mark Johnson, who had joined Chandler's coaching staff in 1982, became head baseball coach. Johnson's teams won the Southwest Conference championship in 1986, 1989, and 1993 and made seven NCAA

James R. ("Randy") Matson set a world shot put record of *71* feet, *5 ½* inches, with this throw in Kyle Field on April *22, 1967*. Courtesy University Studio.

Former Texas A&M football coach Jackie Sherrill led the Aggies to three consecutive Southwest Conference championships and Cotton Bowl appearances. Courtesy Johnson Photography.

In *1993*, John David Crow became director of athletic development. Courtesy Johnson Photography.

Wally Groff, director of athletics. Photograph by James Lyle. Courtesy Texas A&M University Photographic Services.

Texas A&M men's basketball coach Tony Barone. Courtesy Johnson Photography.

Texas A&M head baseball coach Mark Johnson has led the Aggies to three Southwest Conference championships. Courtesy Johnson Photography.

The *1993* Southwest Conference championship baseball team. Front row, left to right: *Manager Joel Wellman, Manager Neil Nugent, Manager Mike Delesandri, David Martin, Jason Washburn, Robert Harris, Jim Hicks, Eric Gonzalez, Manager David Marek, Manager Perry Rollen, Manager Kyle Wohlfahrt, Student Trainer Rob Redding;* second row: *Assistant Head Coach Jon Peters, Rob Thomas, Kevin Bosse, David Minor, Lee Fedora, Robert Lewis, Stephen Claybrook, Brian Johnson, Jason Chesson, Student Assistant Coach Tim Prichard, Volunteer Assistant Coach David Crowson, Head Coach Mark Johnson, Assistant Coach Bill Hickey;* third row: *Brian Bittiker, Brian Thomas, Spencer McIntyre, Rob Trimble, Matt Miller, Chad Alexander, Jeff Jansky, Trey Moore;* back row: *Jason Stephens, Brian Parker, John Codrington, Chris Clemons, Matt Sherwood, Kelly Wunsch, Jeff Granger, Ryan Langston, Scott Smith, Billy Harlan, John Curl. Courtesy Johnson Photography.*

regional appearances. Johnson achieved a remarkable .719 winning record during those years, and Aggie baseball became a major spectator sport. Olsen field was enlarged in 1995 to accommodate the growing attendance.

Since the organization of competitive intercollegiate track teams by Texas A&M in 1902, Aggies have produced some outstanding teams. They won the Southwest Conference eleven times between 1915 and 1970. All-time great track men include the following:

Jack Mahan:	1920 Olympic Team (5th in javelin)
Roy Bucek:	1942 All-America (hurdles)
Pete Watkins:	1942 All-America (high jump)
Jitterbug Henderson:	1943 All-America (javelin)
Art Harnden:	1946 All-America (440 dash), 1948 All-America (440 dash), 1948 Olympic Team (1st in 1600-meter relay)
George Kaders:	1948 All-America (discus)
Walt Davis:	1951 All-America (high jump), 1952 All-America (high jump), 1952 Olympic Team (1st in high jump), 1952 World Record (6'11 ½" in high jump)
Darrow Hooper:	1951 All-America (shot put), 1952 All-America (shot put), 1952 Olympic Team (2nd in shot put), 1953 All-America (shot put)
Bobby Ragsdale:	1953 All-America (broad jump)
Randy Matson:	1964 All-America (shot put), 1964 Olympic Team (2nd in shot put), 1965 All-America (shot put), 1965 World Record (shot put), 1966 All-America (shot put and discus), 1967 World Record (71' 5 ½" in shot put), 1968 Olympic Team (1st in shot put).

In 1969, four A&M men made All-America. Curtis Mills won the NCAA meet with the world record of 44.7 in the 440-yard dash. Jack Abbott, Scott Hendricks, and Rockie Woods joined Mills on the 440-yard relay team that swept All-America honors with a time of 39.5 seconds.

In 1970, Mills ran the anchor leg on A&M's world record-setting 880-yard and mile relays. Rockie Woods was Southwest Conference champion in the 100-meter dash in 1969, 1970, and 1971. Tony Wheeler topped the Southwest Conference in the 800-meter in 1976. Later, in 1978, 1979, and 1980, Curtis Dickey won three straight NCAA championships in the 60-meter dash. High jumper Jimmy Howard, marathon competitor Kyle Heffner, and Linda Waltman in the pentathlon were selected for the U.S. Olympic team (which declined the invitation to participate in Moscow). Rod Richardson a four-time All-American, won the NCAA title in the 60-meter dash in 1982 with a collegiate record time of 6.07. Arturo Barrios, who took the 10,000-meter championship in 1984, was Southwest Conference champion in the 5,000- and 10,000-meter runs in 1985 and All-American in the 10,000.

Other 1980s All-American tracksters included Stanley Kerr and Floyd Heard (200-meter); Leslie Kerr and Howard Davis (400-meter); Lawrence Felton and Richard Bucknor (110-meter hurdles); Billy Busch, Chappelle Henderson, and Craig Calk (400-meter hurdles); Jimmy Howard (high jump); Ian James (long jump); and Francisco Olivares (triple jump). Robert Graf took All-American in the discus in 1989, and Juan de la Garza received the honor in the javelin in 1983. Randy Hall captured All-American honors in pole vaulting from 1979 to 1981, while Greg West closed the decade an All-American in indoor pole vaulting for 1988 and 1990.

In the tradition set by Olympic champion Randy Matson, shotputter Randy Barnes won the silver at the 1988 Olympics, and Mike Stulce captured the gold in 1992. In 1991, Andre Cason helped the U.S. 400-meter relay team take the world championship title and set a new world record of 37.50, and the next year Cason set a world record in the 60-meter dash, bettering his own record a month later. Richard Bucknor won the All-American title in the 110-meter hurdles in 1990, Gregg Williams in 1991, and Nic Pollard in 1992. Aggies receiving All-American track and field recognition in the 1990s include Scott Paulsen (discus), Ty Sevin (javelin), Richard Murphy (400-meter hurdles), Aaron Ramirez (10,000-meter run), Howard Davis (400-meter dash), and Andre Cason and Gerry Woodberry (100-meter dash).

Texas A&M's track tradition has for the most part been under the tutelage of three coaches: Frank G.

Former Student *Association* Director Randy Matson and Mike Stulce show off their Olympic medals. Matson won the gold in the *1968* Olympics, and Stulce captured the gold in *1992*. Photograph by James Lyle. Courtesy Texas A&M University Photographic Services.

"Andy" Anderson, Charlie Thomas, and Ted Nelson. Anderson, who was variously commandant and coach in the 1920s and 1930s, became mayor of College Station. Charlie Thomas presided over the thinclads for thirty-two years, retiring in 1990. Ted Nelson, an A&M All-American who ran under Thomas in the early 1960s, then took over as head track and field coach for Aggie men and women.

In the 1970s, women entered the lists of Aggies competing in track and field events. Linda Waltman paced the Aggie women competitors with record times in the 100- and 200-meter dash between 1977 and 1979. She became A&M's first female All-American in 1988. In 1980, she was selected for the Olympic pentathlon competition, but the U.S. boycotted the Moscow games. Novaita Samuels stepped in to head up Aggie women competitors in 1982 and 1983, earning All-American honors in the 100-meter dash in 1982. Judy Williams, Kasandra McDaniel, Rosalyn Hunt, Regina Gentry, and Trisha Harris were among the top women performers of the 1980s, in the 400-meter and shorter races. Suzanne Sheffield led Aggie women in the 800-, 1500-, and 3000-meter runs in the early 1980s. Barb Collingsworth, Lori Scott, Stacy

Head track and field coach Ted Nelson, with assistant coach Juan De La Garza. Courtesy Johnson Photography.

Anjanette Kirkland competing in the 100-meter hurdles. Courtesy Johnson Photography.

Ware, and Marilee Matheny were among top performers in the distance races. Aggie women turned in winning heats in the long jump, triple jump, discus, javelin, and shot put. Many received All-American recognition:

1978	Linda Waltman	Pentathlon
1979	Linda Waltman	Pentathlon
1980	Vickilee Coburn	Discus
1981	Ellen Smith	400-Meter Hurdles
1982	Novaita Samuels	100-Meter Dash
1982	Novaita Samuels	200-Meter Dash
1982	Marilee Matheny	10,000-Meter Run
1983	Suzanne Sheffield	800-Meter Run
1984	Sandra Cooper	400-Meter Dash (Indoor)
1987	Judy Williams	200-Meter Dash
1988	Alissa Bell	Long Jump
1988	Melinda Clark	High Jump
1989	Melinda Clark	High Jump
1989	Yolanda Taylor	Long Jump
1989	Yolanda Taylor	Triple Jump
1990	Sandra Hines	High Jump
1991	Yolanda Taylor	Long Jump
1991	Gwen Buck	High Jump
1992	Rosa Baker	100-Meter Hurdles
1992	Twylana Harrison	Triple Jump
1993	Anjanette Kirkland	100-Meter Hurdles
1993	Kalleen Madden	Heptathlon
1994	Anjanette Kirkland	100-Meter Hurdles
1994	Michelle Stirrett	Javelin
1995	Anjanette Kirkland	55-Meter Hurdles

In addition, Ellen Smith, Evelyn Smith, Sandra Cooper, and Novaita Samuels won All-American honors in the 400- and 1,600-meter relays in 1982.

Women's athletics were placed under Southwest Conference Athletic Association rules for the first time in 1982. Aggie women's softball teams took national titles in 1982, 1983, and 1987. Lynn Hickey joined the coaching staff as women's head basketball coach in 1984. Hickey took the Aggie women from obscurity to national prominence during ten seasons, with an overall win-loss record of 154-128. She accepted the position as senior associate athletic director in 1994 after closing a 23-8 season and taking second in the Southwest Conference. Candi Harvey, a former head coach from Tulane University, took over the coaching job, foreseeing a bright future for the lady Aggie netters: "With the right mix of good health, good luck, and great confidence, anything can happen." For women's sports at Texas A&M University, it already has happened.

Other sports also have received their share of interest and participation at A&M. Tennis appeared at the turn of the century, and boxing was introduced on the campus in 1917.

Soccer, which first appeared in 1918, has experienced a come-back in recent years. Swimming came of age at A&M in 1934, the same year the P. L. Downs Natatorium opened. Swimming teams coached by Arthur D. Adamson produced five All-America swimmers. His teams won the Southwest Conference title in 1946 and 1956 and shared the title in 1944.

The building program at A&M has reflected athletic concerns on campus. DeWare Field House was constructed in 1924. A&M's first concrete tennis courts were built in 1946. An eighteen-hole golf course was

After coaching the women's basketball team for ten years, Lynn Hickey became senior associate athletic director in 1994. Courtesy Texas A&M University Archives.

Lady Aggies coach Candi Harvey. Courtesy Johnson Photography.

opened in 1950 and was completely renovated in 1974. Henderson Hall, a dormitory for freshmen and varsity athletes, was completed in 1958. The building was named for Robert William ("Jitterbug") Henderson ('42), a great all-around Aggie athlete who earned eleven letters in five major sports. It was replaced by a modern new athletic dormitory complex that was completed in 1974. The new structure was named for

Wofford Cain ('13) of Dallas, a loyal fan and substantial supporter of A&M athletic programs. In August, 1995, a new sports recreation center opened its doors, offering students everything from swimming to rock climbing. Through thick and thin, Aggies yesterday and today are unexcelled in their support for their teams.

The Student Recreation Center, a *286,000* square foot intramural, fitness, and health center, opened in August, *1995*, and offers everything from mountain climbing to aerobics. Photograph by James Lyle. Courtesy Texas A&M University Photographic Services.

*"Texas A&M had truly come a long way,
but the next fifty years would bring even
more profound changes."*

Thomas O. Walton, president, *1925–43*. Courtesy Texas A&M University Archives.

Kyle Field encompasses almost a hundred years of history, excitement, and Aggie spirit. Courtesy Texas A&M University Photographic Services.

Receiving help from a fellow *Aggie*, a senior cadet finds a new way to wade through Fish Pond during Elephant walk. Photograph by Mike Kellett. Courtesy Texas *A&M* University Photographic Services.

Reveille VI assumed authority from a long line of predecessors dating back to *1935*. Photograph by Mike Kellett. Courtesy Texas *A&M* University Photographic Services.

*Sports events have always seemed to be
more than just athletic contests at A&M—
whether it's football, baseball, track, or soccer,
Aggie pride is on hand to lend a unique quality
to the color and excitement of the game . . .*

The Corps of Cadets stand tall during pre-game ceremonies at Kyle Field. Courtesy Texas A&M University Photographic Services.

Bucky Richardson, former A&M quarterback, always dazzled the fans with his athletic abilities. Courtesy Johnson Photography.

Ask someone if he's an Ex-Aggie
and he'll likely tell you no ...
that there isn't any such thing as an Ex-Aggie ...

Football, which drove the people "hog wild" in the *1890s*, continues to enthrall and excite Aggies in the *1990s*. Courtesy Texas A&M University Photographic Services.

R. C. Slocum (center) holds the record as the "winningest" coach in Southwest Conference history (including three consecutive Southwest Conference championships in *1991*, *1992*, and *1993*)—a record that, with the dissolution of the Southwest Conference, will never be broken. Photograph by Mike Kellett. Courtesy Texas A&M University Photographic Services.

In *1978*, A&M dedicated its new baseball field to C. E. "Pat" Olsen, a *1923* graduate and a member of the legendary New York Yankees team which fielded such immortals as Babe Ruth and Lou Gehrig. Photograph by Mike Kellett. Courtesy Texas A&M University Photographic Services.

... it's not something you are for three or four years, and then suddenly aren't anymore ...

Trey Moore (left) waves Billy Harlan home. Photograph by Mike Kellett. Courtesy Texas A&M University Photographic Services.

Texas A&M's Tony McGinnis takes it to the hoop against the University of Texas. Courtesy Johnson Photography.

With the centerpole in place, *Aggies* begin work on the first "stack," carrying on a tradition began at the turn of the twentieth century. Photograph by Mike Kellett. Courtesy Texas A&M University Photographic Services.

The bonfire symbolizes the *Aggies*' "burning desire to beat the hell out of t.u." and signifies the *Aggies*' great love for their school. Photograph by Mike Kellett. Courtesy Texas A&M University Photographic Services.

VIII.

Fifty Years and Counting

The first decade of A&M's second half-century began auspiciously with the "Semi-Centennial Celebration and the Inauguration of Thomas Otto Walton, LL.D., as President of the College." "Anniversary Day" and the inauguration, by declaration of the board, was set for Saturday, October 16, 1926. This date was fifty years and twelve days after the dedication ceremonies, on that barren windswept knoll, when Governor Richard Coke and President Thomas S. Gathright hailed the birth of Texas' first public institution of higher learning.

Texas A&M had truly come a long way, but the next fifty years would bring even more profound changes.

The College's endowment was substantially enriched by the discovery of oil on University lands. Oil revenues were eventually prorated between the University of Texas and Texas A&M.

President Thomas O. Walton's administration (1925–43) was early destined to be one of persisting crisis. There was a depression in the offing. And war. It was a time of change, growth, and turbulence. A great building program began. Three new dormitories were dedicated in 1927. Directors let the contract for the E. B. Cushing Library. The College ROTC program added a unit of engineers in 1927. In 1929, a curriculum in petroleum engineering was established at the request of the oil industry. Directors again investigated the perennial hazing problem in 1928, and

in 1929 they prohibited the practice of having freshmen clean the rooms of upperclassmen. They also banned "fish calls," which involved rousing the entire freshman class at odd and uninviting hours for unusual, and usually uninviting, tasks. In the 1930s—by action of the board, through the declaration of the courts, and with the approval of most former students—the modern era at Texas A&M was reserved exclusively for men. It was to remain so for almost another half-century.

Throughout the twenties and thirties the A&M Board was partially preoccupied with business—oil leases, building contracts, deposits, interest rates, bonds, and fiscal controls. These were days when money was especially important, and in short supply.

With the end of World War I, some degree of laxity crept into the military regimen of the College. Veterans were exempted from the Corps of Cadets. A number of women attended classes. Foreign students and graduate students appeared in increasing numbers, and some regular students displayed a distinct aversion to the military system. In order to clarify the matter, the directors issued a statement in May, 1930, reaffirming the military character of the school: all nonmilitary students who lived in dormitories, except graduate students or foreign students and those physically unable to perform military duties, would be required to wear the regulation uniform with some insignia to indicate they were not members of the

The "Horse Soldiers," *1924–25. Courtesy Texas A&M University Archives.*

Aggies at Summer Camp, *1935. Courtesy Texas A&M University Archives.*

Fish Day in *1933. Courtesy Texas A&M University Archives.*

Reveille I, in 1935. Courtesy Texas A&M University Archives.

The Ring Dance, 1936. Courtesy Texas A&M University Archives.

ROTC. They would be organized into companies and placed in charge of a civilian supervisor who would maintain orderly conduct and who would have general charge of the group.

The military position of the College had changed little since 1876. Times, however, had changed. The old question of admitting women to Texas A&M arose with fresh urgency in the 1920s and 1930s. Few women attended college in those days, and fewer still pursued instruction in the then "unfeminine" fields of farming and engineering. While the first catalog of the College announced admission of only male students fourteen years of age or older, the issue of coeducation seemingly never arose during the first two decades, because no women applied for admission. It was generally accepted that Texas A&M was an all-male school.

In the 1890s, public interest in coeducation at A&M arose when the state began serious consideration of founding a girls' industrial school. President Sul Ross was reportedly besieged by promoters of this institution, who desired to incorporate the school under the auspices of the A&M Board. Ross responded favorably, even to the point of recommending the school be located on the campus with A&M.

Interest in a female institution heightened over the next few years, especially among the businessmen and citizens of Bryan, who recognized the economic opportunities inherent in a new school. Also, many of these citizens desired to secure a college education for their daughters. In 1899, a special committee of citizens headed a local effort to locate the proposed school at A&M. A brochure stressed the economic advantages to be derived from the use of mutual facilities and faculty and the "refining influence" of the young ladies upon the boys at A&M.

The Senate passed a bill favoring College Station as a location for the school, but the bill failed to win approval in the House. Finally, in 1901, the legislature approved a bill creating the "Texas Industrial Institute and College for the Education of White Girls of the State of Texas in the Arts and Sciences" under a separate board of regents, to be located by a special commission appointed by the governor. Thus, Texas Women's University, in Denton, came to be a "sister" school rather than a part of Texas A&M.

In 1915, the board made its first official policy statement excluding women from regular sessions at A&M. Despite this ruling, time and circumstances continued to promote a certain amount of flexibility in the all-male rule.

Final Review, a proud tradition—about 1930. Courtesy Texas A&M University Archives.

A&M commencement ceremonies in the early 1930s. Courtesy Texas A&M University Archives.

Fish Day in 1933. Courtesy Texas A&M University Archives.

The cavalry stands ready, early 1930s. Courtesy Texas A&M University Archives.

After World War I, married veterans brought their wives to the campus, and provisions were made for many of them to attend classes as "special unofficial students."

Seven women attended in 1922, fourteen in 1923. Thirty were enrolled by 1925 when President William Bennett Bizzell departed. Bizzell saw "no reason for not admitting a reasonable number of girls to this institution, especially the daughters of employees of the College . . . and mature young people who sought the particular advantages offered by this College." Under Bizzell's leadership, A&M appeared to be moving very gradually toward a coeducational status. But even the postwar trend to admit women and the open-door attitude of Bizzell failed to convert the school into a coeducational institution.

In 1925, directors ruled that "only relatives of college employees and women who seek special education unavailable elsewhere" should be admitted. The directors completely reversed their deci-sion soon after as too liberal and ruled that "no girls should ever be admitted to the College." Then, some-time later, they realized this flat statement contradicted the law requiring the admission of women in summer school, and made that exception to the rule.

From 1925 until 1933, no women attended classes

Aggies and their dates pose for a formal portrait at the *1934* Spring Dance. Courtesy Texas A&M University Archives.

Aggies at Summer Camp, *1934*. Courtesy Texas A&M University Archives.

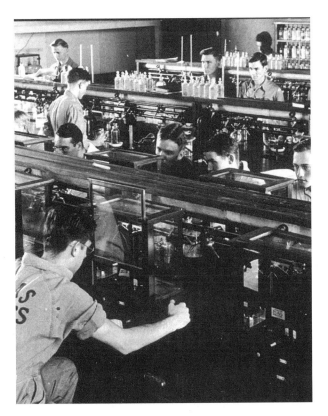

The A&M chemistry lab, *1934*. Courtesy Texas A&M University Archives.

The Aggie bonfire was a glorified junk pile in *1934*. Courtesy Texas A&M University Archives.

Shades of things to come—a parking problem at Kyle Field, 1935. Courtesy Texas A&M University Archives.

as special or regular students. By 1933, however, as the depression deepened and faculty salaries were lowered by 25 percent, the directors eased the "men only" ruling to allow daughters of faculty and staff to enroll.

This sprung the lid of Pandora's box. If daughters of faculty could attend, why not daughters of other local townsmen or Texans anywhere? A number of Bryan girls applied and were categorically denied admission.

Local parents filed a writ. Eventually, the case was heard, and Judge William C. Davis concluded:

> . . . if the Legislature had seen fit to declare in specific language the status of all the other institutions of learning . . . with respect to the admission of both sexes, and with reference to A&M it remains silent, the only logical conclusion that can be reached is that the Legislature intended to leave to the discretion of the Board of Directors of the College the admission of girls and women.

For two more decades the old issue of coeducation lay dormant. It arose again with new vigor in 1953. Finally, in 1963, a different resolution began to emerge. One impact of the "men only" policy during the next several decades may have been, as a faculty-staff-student survey reported in 1962, that the exclusion of women impeded the development of academic excellence at A&M and, as some argued, slowed the rate of enrollment growth. The rapid growth of enrollment at Texas A&M in the 1970s can be attributed in good part to a large enrollment by women, accommodated by new dormitories for women, and the creation of the office of dean of women.

During the 1920s and 1930s, fighting flared over the distribution of funds from the permanent university fund. In the past, the problem of dividing money had failed to be overly critical—largely because money from University lands was nominal and came mostly from surface leases and land sales.

SANTA RITA CHANGED ALL THAT.

Santa Rita was a discovery oil field located on University lands that came into production in 1923. By 1926, oil royalties flowing into the permanent university fund reached $250,000 per month, and total royalties accumulated by that time equaled more than $5 million. Texas A&M's "share" was now a horse of a different color.

A&M resolved to seek an out-of-court settlement of the matter with the University of Texas regents. Failing that, they would take the school's case for a share in the revenues to court.

Initial negotiations led nowhere. Several years passed without any agreement, and, in 1929, A&M directors determined to seek legal resolution.

A&M directors and University regents met again in 1930. In March, A&M received and approved recommendations of a joint committee on revenue which provided that A&M would receive $100,000 for four years and thereafter would receive one-third of the royalties from University lands. On the same day, Texas regents rejected the agreement. Finally, a revised proposal offered A&M $150,000 for the fiscal year, ending August 31, 1931, and for the next three fiscal years. Beginning September 1, 1934, A&M would receive one-third of the income of the permanent university fund, excluding income from surface leases, which was to be reserved to the University. The A&M directors and the Texas regents approved this proposal.

Both schools, and higher education in Texas, stood to benefit by an agreement for the division of University endowment funds and the removal of legislative restrictions on the use of those funds. Without doubt, the outstanding factor that has made Texas higher education effective and competent, if not outstanding, has been the availability of vast and essentially unrestricted sums of money for the use of its major public universities. Few states of the union have so well endowed their institutions of higher learning.

A bill confirming these agreements, only slightly altered, was passed by the Texas Legislature in 1931. The impact of this new source of money on Texas A&M was immediate. Results were even more spectacular. Between 1929 and 1937, the years of most severe depression, A&M spent over $3 million on construction, an amount almost equal to the total spent on capital improvements during the school's first fifty years.

During these same years, enrollment increased from about three to five thousand students. Such growth could not have occurred without available endowment funds.

The building program of this era had, in addition to the physical improvement of A&M facilities, yet another intangible and symbolic effect on the College. Texas A&M turned away from the railroad and the west, leaving its pioneering days behind. It faced a new highway, the east, and a new age of growth.

In 1932, directors let the contract for the new administration building, the systems building, which served as the gateway to the university for the next four decades, until it too became symbolically overshadowed by the skyscraper, space-age structures of the 1970s.

When the stock market crashed on October 24, 1929, financial panic shook the nation—including College Station. Banks were forced to close, and factories and businesses went under. Consumers quit buying. Farmers, caught since 1921 in a depression

of their own, found no market for their crops. Foreclosures and hard times hit rural areas. Unemployment spiraled from 1.5 million in 1929 to over 12 million in 1932.

THIS WAS THE GREAT DEPRESSION!

Compared with other areas and other people, the impact of the depression at A&M was mild. A&M actually did marvelously well in many respects, largely due to the flow of royalty money that began in 1932. Still, compared with normal times, A&M, too, suffered. In 1931, the board held an emergency meeting to consider how A&M funds and investments might best be protected. Enrollment dropped because parents simply lacked the cash to send their boys to college.

Project houses, or student cooperatives, helped some students remain at school. Groups of boys rented a house, pooled their money, brought food from home or the farm, and learned they could live more cheaply than they could on campus. In 1933 and 1934, more project houses were begun under the board's "exceptions in exceptional cases" rule, allowing more students to live off campus. Additionally, in 1937, the College authorized construction contracts for fourteen project buildings from institutional funds. By the end of the year, over fifty project houses were in operation on and off campus.

The student co-op idea spread from A&M to the University of Texas campus, and the plan was picked up by a number of schools around the country. The project-house program demonstrated that Aggies were industrious and conscientious students, and it reflected the deep and genuine commitment of students, faculty, and administrators to higher education.

In May, 1931, the legislature authorized the organization and establishment of a nautical school, to be under the control of Texas A&M, to instruct boys "in seamanship, ship construction, naval architecture, wireless telegraph, engineering and the science of navigation." The bill had a curious proviso, in that the state declared it would never be called upon to appropriate money for support of the school. Almost three decades later the proviso was repealed, and the Texas Maritime Academy was established. It became a part of Texas A&M University's Moody College of Marine Sciences and Maritime Resources, and, in 1972, Texas A&M was designated a "Sea Grant College." The depression, however, had effectively postponed A&M's march to the sea for a while.

The darkest days of the depression came in 1933. A number of staff positions were eliminated. Other

A field artilleryman takes a sighting, about 1933. Courtesy Texas A&M University Archives.

Old Aggies will remember a "ratted" room—about 1935. Courtesy Texas A&M University Archives.

The signal corps learns its trade. Courtesy Texas A&M University Archives.

workers were given salary cuts. The legislature approved a 25 percent across-the-board salary reduction for all state employees, including college teachers. New economies effected in 1935 included the discontinuance of the School of Vocational Teaching.

In 1936, a retirement program was instituted to provide additional benefits to the faculty. The program provided for retirement at the age of seventy.

Perhaps the most critical phenomenon of the Great Depression at A&M was the fact that large numbers of students had no jobs waiting for them after graduation. The class of 1932 was the hardest hit. Only one engineer in the class had a job at commencement. New government jobs became available with the New Deal recovery agencies, and a gradual upswing in business improved the employment picture. Throughout the thirties, however, any job at all—at almost any salary—was welcomed by the graduate.

In 1931, the Forty-first Legislature created the office of state auditor and efficiency expert. The Forty-

Silver Taps in 1935. Courtesy Texas A&M University Archives.

second Legislature, pressed for funds, resolved to study ways of implementing economies in government and ways of deriving new avenues of income. A joint com-

Final Review, about 1935. Courtesy Texas A&M University Archives.

mittee compiled its report, called the Griffenhagen Report. The document was highly critical of the Texas A&M academic program and of the administration of the A&M system. Recommendations proposed shocking changes: that the functions of the board be transferred to a proposed state board of education; that A&M discontinue offering degrees in arts and sciences; that A&M offer degrees only in agriculture. A great many other extreme changes were proposed. If many of the recommendations had been effected, there might be little left of A&M today. Fortunately, few of the advised changes ever came to pass. A number of the recommended changes were made, but not quite in the manner the report advised.

In the thirties, many men who later would take higher posts were already making their mark at A&M. Frank Cleveland Bolton, who would become president of A&M in 1948, was climbing from head of the Department of Electrical Engineering to dean of engineering, to acting dean of the College in 1931. Gibb Gilchrist, who became president in 1944, was dean of the School of Engineering in 1937.

The directors created the Department of Wild Game in 1937. The Department of Aeronautical Engineering was created in 1939, and the Department of Industrial Engineering came into being that same year.

During the depression, Texas A&M had evidently placed too much of its money in buildings and too little in people, creating a condition which was chronic well into the postwar years. An administrative and academic reorganization begun in 1937 did much to improve the situation. State appropriations increased

in 1937, and salary raises were received by key administrators. However, raises were not passed down in significant number to the faculty.

In 1936, the board authorized the granting of the regular Doctor of Philosophy (Ph.D.) degree and the granting of the Doctor of Science in agriculture and engineering. Twelve new dormitories and a mess hall were named in recognition of those who had served the College with distinction. A new civil engineering building was completed. An electrical engineering building was constructed.

The memorial gymnasium was renamed Charlie Deware Field House in 1939, in honor of one of A&M's outstanding athletes. Guion Hall was outfitted for motion pictures.

Gibb Gilchrist, newly appointed dean of engineering, applied to the CAA for certification of Texas A&M to give primary flight training and primary and secondary ground-school courses. Certification was approved. Texas A&M became one of the few colleges in the country to own an airport facility. The Jesse E. Easterwood Airport was formally dedicated on May 22, 1941. Jesse Easterwood left A&M in 1917 to enlist in the Naval Air Service, received a commission as ensign, and won promotion to the rank of lieutenant. He served with the British Royal Flying Corps in 1918 and completed sixteen successful raids behind German lines. He was killed in a plane accident in the Canal Zone, May 19, 1919, and was posthumously awarded the Navy Cross.

College Station, which had originated as a "flag station" on the old Houston and Texas Central Rail-

President Franklin D. Roosevelt visited the campus on May *11, 1937*, and congratulated the cadets on A&M's outstanding record in World War I, soon to be surpassed in World War II. Courtesy Texas A&M University Archives.

A&M's Easterwood Airport was named in honor of World War I pilot Jesse L. Easterwood (*'09*). Courtesy Texas A&M University Archives.

The "new" Corps dorms, about *1940*. Courtesy Texas A&M University Archives.

The president's home, erected in *1891*, was originally a "gingerbread" mansion. Completely remodeled about *1930*, it remained in use until it burned in January, *1963*. Courtesy Texas A&M University Archives.

The college bugler gave the call to classes, meals, study, and bed. Reveille I, pictured here about 1938, assisted. Courtesy Texas A&M University Archives.

road in 1876, became an incorporated city under the General Laws of the State of Texas in 1938. The development of an incorporated town relieved the College of one of its greatest burdens, that of housing its own personnel.

By 1941, the depression was over. It left a number of interesting legacies at Texas A&M. There were more buildings and lower salaries, more students and fewer courses, an airport, a nonfunded maritime academy, project houses, government projects, an incorporated town, a legislative committee indictment, and school spirit unparalleled in the history of the College.

THEN CAME WORLD WAR II!

"In humble reverence ... to those men of A&M
who gave their lives in defense of our country ...
their sacrifices shall not be forgotten."

The war clouds in September, *1939*, grew darker as Nazi Germany and Russia
carved up Poland. One year later the United States began to mobilize the National
Guard. Two years later, September, *1941*, France had fallen and the Battle of
Britain raged. Courtesy Confederate Air Forces Flying Museum.

IX.

World War II:
The Fighting Texas Aggies

Men from Texas A&M fought and died on every battle-field of World War II. The school, said Douglas MacArthur, commander of American forces in the Pacific in 1942, "is writing its own military history in the blood of its graduates." In 1946, Dwight D. Eisenhower, chief of staff, said:

> No more convincing testimony could be given to the manner in which the men of Texas A&M lived up to the ideals and principles inculcated in their days on the campus than the simple statement that the Congressional Medal of Honor has been awarded to six former students, that 46 took part in the heroic defense of Bataan and Corregidor and that nearly 700 are on the list of our battle dead.

Almost twenty thousand Texas A&M former students served in the armed forces during World War II. Some fourteen thousand of these were officers, twenty-nine in the rank of general. Texas A&M furnished more officers than the United States Military Academy at West Point.

Aggies were at Pearl Harbor, Bataan, Corregidor, Midway, Guadalcanal, with James Doolittle over Tokyo, at Normandy, in North Africa and Italy, and at the Battle of the Bulge.

"The men of Texas A&M," General Omar Bradley told the graduating class of 1950, "can stand up to any men in the world and compare favorably their education and training for leadership—leadership in the pursuits of peace, and if it comes to war, leadership in battle."

The United States, said Franklin D. Roosevelt, "hates war" and "hopes for peace." But while the American Congress debated neutrality legislation, it authorized the rearmament of America for war. In September, 1940, Congress, at the urging of the president, passed the Selective Service Act. The war's imminence was felt at A&M in early 1939, when the board of directors authorized President Thomas O. Walton to offer the services of the College to the national government in any needed capacity. Pointing to the necessities of national defense, in late spring Texas A&M launched a campaign urging Texas high school boys to attend a military college.

Charles Monroe ("Tennessee") Johnson, who graduated in June, 1939, was probably the first Aggie to go to war. He felt so strongly about Hitler's aggression in Europe that in May, 1940, he temporarily renounced his American citizenship, hitchhiked to Canada, and joined the Canadian Seaforths. He served with that unit for the next five and one-half years.

In September, 1940, as National Guard units began to be called to active duty, students began to leave the campus. The College returned all unspent fees to those called to duty. Ross Hall was repaired and converted to the use of the military science program. The directors authorized a short course in chemical warfare.

In June, 1941, while Hitler's armies rolled through France, the A&M Board of Directors went on record in support of a bill to provide universal military training. Thus, by late 1941, Texas A&M was as well-prepared—or as ill-prepared—for war as the rest of the nation.

Suddenly, on Sunday, December 7, 1941, Texas A&M, along with the rest of the country, was swept into the whirlwind of war. The campus was quiet that Sunday afternoon. Many students were at the Campus Theater watching *A Yank in the R.A.F.* The film snapped, and amidst the proverbial catcalls and boos, theater manager Charlie Tiegner announced, "If you would care to know, Japanese forces have just bombed Pearl Harbor."

There was shocked disbelief, followed by yells of "Beat the hell out of Japan!" "Let's take a corps trip to Tokyo!"

Many Aggies were already nearly that close to the heart of the Japanese Empire—prominently at Corregidor, Bataan, Mindanao, and Midway.

President Roosevelt, on December 8, 1941, asked Congress for a declaration of war against Japan; that afternoon the Academic Council of Texas A&M, representing the faculty and administration, adopted a resolution extending all facilities of the College to the national government for the war effort. President Walton and Colonel Maurice D. Welty, commandant of the Corps of Cadets, meanwhile urged all students to remain at school. "When your country needs you, it will call," they said.

And it did. Some, to be sure, had already been called. Among these was Maj. Gen. George Moore. When Moore, commandant of the Corps of Cadets and a 1908 A&M graduate, left College Station in 1940, he selected thirty-five graduating Aggies to precede him to his new post in the Philippines. When the Japanese invaded the Philippines in December, 1941, American forces retreated into the Bataan Peninsula across the bay from Manila. In April of 1942, after a bitter defense and prolonged siege, Bataan fell.

Some survivors managed to cross over to the adjoining American fortress of Corregidor under the command of Lt. Gen. Jonathan M. Wainright, where Maj. Gen. George Moore commanded units at Fort Mills. On April 21, twenty-five Aggies, including Moore, celebrated San Jacinto Day on Corregidor. They drank toasts of water to the Texas heroes of 1836, sang A&M songs, told stories of their college days, and had their "muster" interrupted by Japanese shells. Within two weeks they were dead or imprisoned. Corregidor had fallen.

Col. George F. Moore was Texas A&M commandant from *1938* to *1940*. Courtesy Texas A&M University Archives.

Thus was formed the Corregidor Chapter of the Former Students of the Agricultural and Mechanical College of Texas. The Aggies at Corregidor were commemorated by Congress in 1942 and by the initiation of a unique and now traditional muster ceremony on the College Station campus in 1943. In these ceremonies a poem written by Dr. John Ashton ('06) of the Department of Rural Sociology was read to the assembled cadets. As the names of the heroes of Corregidor were read that day, a friend and comrade answered the roll call, "Here!" So the former men of A&M live on in A&M tradition.

The desperate defense by American forces in the South Pacific also involved A&M men in action at Mindanao, the Coral Sea, and Midway. In early 1942, James Connally ('32), a cousin of then Texas Senator Tom Connally, led a bombing mission of five planes from Java to Mindanao through violent weather, sank a Japanese freighter in the midst of a convoy, and landed on Mindanao to rescue twenty-three stranded American pilots. Connally received the Distinguished Service Cross for the action. He died later in combat over Yokohama, Japan. In 1949, the old Waco Army Air Field was renamed James Connally Air Force Base in his honor. Connally's brother, Clem ('38), received the Navy Cross in 1942 for his action as

The Japanese attack on Pearl Harbor almost cleared the Pacific of effective American resistance to Japanese units. Courtesy Purnell Commercial.

Fifteen days before the fall of Corregidor in *1942*, Maj. Gen. George F. Moore and twenty-five of his former A&M students held a muster under the guns of Japanese attackers. Pictured here is the muster held at the same site on April *21*, *1946*. Courtesy Texas A&M University Archives.

a dive-bomber pilot in the battle of the Coral Sea.

At the battle of Midway in 1942, Capt. Charles Gregory ('38) flew fifty-seven combat hours in four days.

In that same battle George H. Gay ('40) flew a Navy torpedo plane and was the only survivor of Torpedo Squadron 8. During the war he won the Navy Cross, with air medal, and several citations for bravery.

The entire Aggie class of *1941* entered military service en masse in May, *1941*. The following year the *1942* class also entered en masse. Courtesy Association of Former Students.

Capt. John I. Hopkins, Jr. ('40), flew bomber missions against German columns in the Egyptian desert.

By October of 1942, about 6,500 Aggies were in service. Most of them were officers, and twenty-three were known to have been decorated for bravery. A number of Aggies participated in one of the most daring events of the early years of the war—Gen. James Doolittle's April, 1942, raid on Tokyo. Maj. John A. Hilger ('32) was Doolittle's second-in-command.

At home there was considerable confusion and a lack of "war planning" during the first years of conflict. At A&M, there was less planning and more "response" to needs and situations. The most critical need, of course, was manpower for the armed forces.

As an initial response to this need, A&M officials placed the institution and its branches on a three-semester basis of sixteen weeks each for a twelve-month school year, allowing students to earn degrees in three rather than four calendar years. Also, directors authorized the establishment of the first military training program on campus, a program to train 2,050 airmen in air navigation and as bombardiers. Texas A&M's great contribution to the war effort included not only sending its students to war, but training nearly forty-five thousand personnel for all branches of the service.

As a part of the war program at A&M, discipline was tightened, physical training increased, and the "indoctrination" of freshmen relaxed. The minimum

Capt. James T. Connally ('32), posthumous recipient of the Distinguished Service Cross for action against the Japanese in *1942*. James Connally Air Force Base, later to become a technical-vocational branch of Texas A&M for a time, was named in his honor. Courtesy Texas A&M University Archives.

A marching scene from the World War II *movie,* We've Never Been Licked, *filmed on the A&M campus in 1943. Reveille I is in the lower right corner. Courtesy Universal Pictures.*

age requirement for appointment as army officers was lowered to eighteen years. A&M's regular ROTC program added a quartermaster corps.

Throughout the early months of the war students were leaving campus to join the services. Others felt confused by the fact that, on the one hand, they were advised to stay in school and continue studies in areas recognized as vital to the national defense, and, on the other hand, if they did remain in school, they often found themselves drafted.

In May, 1942, the War Department organized the Army Enlisted Reserve Corps for college students. Under this plan students could enlist in the services and attend college on an inactive duty status. In theory, those who maintained a good academic record could expect to finish school and be commissioned. In practice, academic studies gave way almost entirely to the necessity of providing manpower for war. In September, 1942, Secretary of War Henry L. Stimson announced that all college-student members of the Enlisted Reserve Corps would be called to active duty when they reached the age of eighteen.

The War Department also soon scrapped advanced ROTC training entirely and substituted the Army Spe-cialized Training Program, which, while conducted on campus, further removed the cadet from civilian study.

In October, 1942, the Former Students Association of Texas A&M addressed a letter to the president of the United States expressing concern over the confusing draft situation and advising the adoption of a coordinated national policy. The letter emphasized that "College men want to do their part to win the war. They should be told what their part is to be, where and how they can best serve, and what their Nation wants and expects them to do." Pointing out various examples of indefinite and changeable programs, the letter concluded that "a total lapse in the college training of men is threatened. If that training is of value in the war program, then action now should be taken to protect and control it."

In January, 1943, however, most doubts about the draft situation had been removed. Everyone available was going to war.

The campus was being rapidly depopulated. In May of that year, within a period of forty-eight hours, the 1,306 juniors and seniors who had been previously inducted left the campus. By February of 1943,

Awarded the Congressional Medal of Honor. Top, 2nd Lieutenant Lloyd D. Hughes ('43); middle, Lieutenant Thomas W. Fowler ('43); bottom, Sergeant George Dennis Keathley ('37). Courtesy Texas A&M University Archives.

Awarded the Congressional Medal of Honor. Top, Lieutenant Turney W. Leonard ('42); middle, Lieutenant Eli Whitely ('41); bottom, Sergeant William Harrell ('43). Courtesy Texas A&M University Archives.

Awarded the Congressional Medal of Honor. Major Horace S. Carswell, Jr. ('38). Courtesy Texas A&M University Archives.

enrollment had already dropped to less than 4,000. By September, it was down to 2,205. In December, only 1,893 students were on campus.

During the early war years the ranks of college professors and employees also declined critically. Soaring salaries in industry attracted many older professors and employees away from the College. As a result, the first real hike in salary levels since the advent of the Great Depression was effected by the board in 1942, in an effort to retain faculty and staff.

Paradoxically, throughout 1944 and 1945, the shortage suddenly turned into a glut as the civilian student body all but disappeared. Some faculty members were returning to their teaching positions only to find they were no longer needed.

Students and faculty put in a six-day work week. Faculty members lectured fifteen to eighteen hours a week, counseled students, graded papers, and worked on special projects and in war drives. The Agricultural Extension Service managed a "Food for Freedom" program designed to increase farm production. The Experiment Station staff taught courses in army mess management. The Army Air Force established its pre-flight training school on campus.

In 1943, a war movie entitled *We've Never Been Licked*

tied the spirit of Aggieland to national defense and became a proud part of the Aggie tradition.

When the first American occupation forces moved into Tokyo after the Japanese surrender in 1945, the first official entry into the city was made by a tank of the First Cavalry Division, emblazoned with the Aggie slogan "We've never been licked" and flying the Texas flag. Texas A&M men, and the Aggie spirit, not only contributed to the war effort in terms of spirit and sheer numbers, but in terms of unexcelled examples of courage and determination. Seven A&M men received the nation's highest decoration, the Congressional Medal of Honor, for their combat service.

Second Lieutenant Lloyd D. Hughes, scheduled for graduation with the class of 1943, volunteered for the Army Air Force. During a grueling and hazardous strategic bombing mission against the refineries at Ploesti, Rumania, Hughes received two direct hits on his B-24 Liberator bombers, lost most of his fuel, and was in flames, but persisted in making his attack. He did so successfully, attempted a crash landing, and was killed on impact, although most of his crew survived. For his heroic action he was posthumously awarded the Medal of Honor.

Lt. Thomas W. Fowler ('43), a tank platoon leader, won the Congressional Medal of Honor for his actions near Corano, Italy, in 1944. Fowler reorganized the remnants of two infantry platoons caught in an enemy mine field. In tank and on foot, he cleared a path through the mine field, even to the point of leaving his tank and pulling up mines with his bare hands, then leading his troops through while under severe enemy fire. His action closed the line and averted what might have been terrible consequences to the entire American force. He emerged untouched from the battle. Ten days later he was killed at the head of his tank platoon when the Fifth Army began its drive on Rome.

After the fall of Rome in June, 1944, Fifth Army units pursued German forces up to the rugged Gothic line in the North Apennine Mountains, where the bitterest fighting of the already bloody Italian campaign ensued. In the attacks on the keystone of the Gothic line, Mount Altruzzo, Sgt. George Dennis Keathley ('35) died in action after so inspiring his men that "they fought with incomparable determination and viciousness." During the last of three consecutive Nazi counterattacks, Keathley gave first aid to the living and collected ammunition from the dead, was mortally wounded by a grenade, and rose up and began firing his rifle, giving orders and encouragement

Ropes and ladder used by Rudder's Rangers on the assault up the Pointe du Hoc cliffs. The first Ranger reached the top of the 100-foot cliffs five minutes after the landing, in the face of small arms fire and "potato masher" grenades dropped by the Germans. Courtesy Texas A&M University Archives.

Lt. Col. James Earl Rudder, commander of the Ranger assault force, June 6, 1944. Of the 225 Rangers who made the attack, only 90 were able to bear arms by the end of the first day. The rest held out against the Germans for two-and-a-half days when finally relieved by reinforcements after repeated German counterattacks. Courtesy Mrs. J. Earl Rudder.

to his men for some fifteen minutes until he dropped dead. He received posthumously the Congressional Medal of Honor.

Lt. Turney W. Leonard, a 1942 A&M graduate, aided his tank destroyer company, a tank company, and 1,100 infantrymen in repelling an attack by two enemy divisions near Kommersheidt, Germany. Leonard's units found themselves trapped in the town by superior German divisions. Leonard and his men held the town and were attacked from three sides. He left his guns to reorganize infantry units and led them in the first attack. Scouting out the enemy alone, he found enemy tanks that were subsequently destroyed. He was wounded many times but returned to his station. During the second and third German attacks, spearheaded by a newly entered German Panzer division, Leonard stood on a "bare blazing hilltop and fought with his guns." Using a submachine gun and grenades, he knocked out a fifty-caliber machine gun, killed sev-

eral enemy snipers, directed fire into a German half-track, and remained in the thick of fighting until a direct shell hit took off the lower part of his arm. "By his superb courage, inspired leadership and indomitable fighting spirit, Lieutenant Leonard enabled our forces to hold the enemy attack and was personally responsible for the direction of fire which destroyed six German tanks." Leonard tied a tourniquet around the stump of his arm and headed for a first-aid station. It was the last time he was ever seen. Capt. Marion C. Pugh ('41), Leonard's commanding officer, later wrote a recommendation for Leonard, "the bravest man I ever saw." He was posthumously awarded the Congressional Medal of Honor.

Lt. Eli Whitely, who finished A&M one year ahead of Turney Leonard, was wounded in the arm and shoulder while leading fifty-five men in house-to-house fighting in Sigolsheim, Germany. He entered a house and killed its two defenders. "Hurling grenades

Mopping-up action on Bougainville, *1944*. The Japanese infiltrated American lines during the night, and at dawn tanks and infantrymen went out to drive them back. Aggies fought in this action and every battle for the Pacific. Courtesy U.S. Army.

Jay T. Robbins (*'40*), later retired as a lieutenant general, USAF, is the leading World War II fighting ace graduated from Texas A&M and the leading living ace from the state of Texas. Courtesy Jay T. Robbins.

before him, he stormed the next house alone and killed two and captured eleven defenders." Later, he rushed into another house, alone, firing his submachine gun, killing five SS troops and capturing twelve. His company captured the village, but not before he was wounded in the eye. For his actions he received the Congressional Medal of Honor. He later returned to A&M to become a professor of agronomy.

Before dawn on March 3, 1945, Sgt. William Harrell, a former A&M student who attended between 1939 and 1941, was on watch near the Nishi Ridge area on Iwo Jima. Japanese forces attacked his position, and a grenade broke his thigh and tore off his left hand. With his right hand he killed a Japanese poised over him with a saber, while another shoved a grenade under his head. Harrell pushed the grenade out, killing another Japanese soldier but losing his other hand. During the attack he killed at least five of the enemy. He was found at dawn, still alive, with a dozen Japanese dead around him. President Harry S. Truman personally awarded Harrell the Medal of Honor.

Maj. Horace S. Carswell, Jr., attended A&M in 1934–35, before transferring to Texas Christian University. During the last year of the war in the Pacific, he served as deputy commander of the 308th Bombardment Group. In a mission to bomb the Japanese shipping

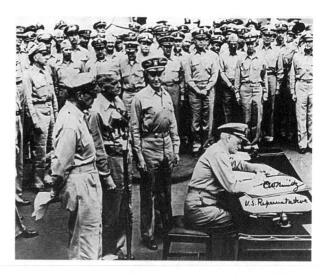

General I. T. Wyche and Olin E. ("Tiger") Teague ('32) along with the Moselle River, Charmes, France, during World War II. Courtesy Texas A&M University Archives.

Colonel Tom Dooley ('35), adjutant to Lieutenant General Jonathan Wainwright, was among those selected to witness the Japanese surrender aboard the U.S.S. Missouri. Admiral C.W. Nimitz is signing the document, with General Douglas MacArthur, Admiral W. F. Halsey, and Rear Admiral Forrest T. Sherman looking on. Courtesy Texas A&M University Archives.

Aggie Muster at Fort Shafter, Honolulu, April 21, 1946. Courtesy Texas A&M University Archives.

This photograph of some of the 288 Americans held at POW Camp No. 1, Fukuoaka, Japan, was taken August 15, 1945, the day after the Japanese commander turned the camp over to Captain Jerome A. McDavitt (top left), senior American officer. This occurred less than a week after atomic bombs were dropped on Hiroshima and Nagasaki and more than three years after McDavitt first became a prisoner of war. Courtesy Jerome McDavitt.

off the coasts of Japan, Carswell's plane was shot to pieces. He gave his life in a supreme effort to save all members of his crew and was posthumously awarded the Medal of Honor. In 1949, Tarrant Field near Fort Worth was renamed in honor of Major Carswell.

Ranger Lt. Col. James Earl Rudder, a graduate of Tarleton Junior College and Texas A&M ('32), was given the job of scaling the cliffs at Pointe du Hoc and destroying an enemy battery of six coastal guns that commanded both American D-Day landing beaches, Utah and Omaha, where at least nineteen other Texas A&M officers with the Second Division accompanied the invasion forces. The cliffs were as high as a nine-story office building. Only thirty minutes were allowed to destroy the six guns. With grappling hooks fired by mortars, Rudder and his men planned to scale the cliffs, but mortars misfired and the ropes on the grapnels were so wet and heavy from seawater that the missiles failed to reach the top of the cliffs. As Rang-

No jubilance, only profound relief, is reflected on the faces of Allied troops witnessing the signature of the U.S. representative accepting the surrender of Japanese commander in the Philippines, General Tomoyuki Yamashita (left foreground, back to camera). The man signing the historic document on September 3, 1945, in Baguio, Luzon, P.I., is Texas A&M former student Major General Edmond H. Leavey ('15). Seated with Major General Leavey on the victors' side of the table are Lieutenant General Jonathan Wainwright (left) and British Lieutenant General Sir Arthur Percival (center), each of whom had suffered greatly at the hands of the Japanese in the Philippines during the three years prior to total surrender. Photograph by P.R.O. AFWESPAC.

Memorial fountain given by the class of '38 in remembrance of those who died in World War II. Photograph by Jerry C. Cooper.

ers clambered up the steep cliffs, German soldiers rolled grenades down on them and cut their lines. Finally, a foothold was gained at the top and the guns were seized and demolished before they could fire at invading forces on the beach. The Rangers held their position for two days. Rudder was wounded twice but remained in command. For that action and later service, Earl Rudder, one day to become president of Texas A&M, won the Distinguished Service Cross, the Legion of Merit, Silver Star, Bronze Star with oak cluster, Purple Heart with oak leaf clusters, French Legion of Honor with croix de guerre and palm, and the Belgian Order of Leopold with croix de guerre and palm.

Lt. Col. Dexter Hodge ('39), a B-24 pilot, earned the Flying Cross, Silver Cross, and Distinguished Service Cross and three oak leaf clusters. Maj. Julian R.

"Softly call the Muster, let comrade answer, 'Here!' Their spirits hover 'round us, as if to bring us cheer!" Courtesy Texas A&M University Archives.

Medal of Honor winner Eli L. Whitely ('41) and President John F. Kennedy, at the military reception at the White House, May 3, 1963. Courtesy Texas A&M University Archives.

This plaque at the Memorial Student Center is a constant reminder of the dedication of men and the sacrifice of war. Photograph by Jerry C. Cooper.

Thornton, Jr. ('40), won the Distinguished Flying Cross and the Air Medal with three oak leaf clusters. Thornton was also a B-24 pilot.

Bergstrom Air Force Base in Austin was named for Aggie J. A. Earl Bergstrom ('29), killed by the Japanese in a bombing raid in Luzon on the second day of the war. Capt. J. Thorpe Robbins ('40), a squadron leader of the "Head Hunters," attached to the Fifth Air Force Fighter Unit on New Guinea, was one of America's leading air aces. By 1944, he had accounted for 18 enemy planes. His squadron had downed a to-

tal of 203. Colonel Carl Storrie ('28), commander of the 318th Bombardment Wing stationed on Guam after its recapture, played an important part in developing low-bombing techniques over Japan. Camp Gary, San Marcos, Texas, was named for Arthur Edward Gary ('40), the first man from San Marcos killed in action in World War II.

For every example of unusual heroism by A&M men in the war, there were a thousand examples of men doggedly and determinedly doing their job. The record of the Fighting Texas Aggies is a proud and extensive part of the record of American fighting men in World War II. The chronicle of the Fighting Texas Aggies will never be fully written, but the sense of achievement and accomplishment has enhanced Aggie tradition with a quiet, proud sense of duty and purposefulness.

Aggies also participated in some of the lighter moments of the conflict. Maj. Archer B. Swank ('36) served as an aide at the Teheran Conference. He recalls that Joseph Stalin looked like an East Texas dirt farmer. He witnessed what may have been the first stubborn impasse between Russia and the West when he noticed Stalin pounding on the bathroom door. "In a moment," said Swank, "with an irate and inquiring expression on his face, out strode Churchill . . ."

Col. Tom Dooley, adjutant to Lt. Gen. Jonathan Wainwright and one of the Aggies taken prisoner on Corregidor, was selected to witness the Japanese surrender aboard the *U.S.S. Missouri* in 1945—a tribute to those who gave so much in the defense of their country.

By war's end, over 950 A&M men had lost their lives in service. These men, whom words are inadequate to describe, will never be forgotten at Texas A&M. In 1951, the Memorial Student Center was dedicated:

In Humble Reverence . . . To Those Men Of A&M Who Gave Their Lives In Defense Of Our Country. Here Is Enshrined In Spirit And In Bronze Enduring Tribute To Their Valor And To Their Devotion. Here Their Memory Shall Remain Forever Fresh—Their Sacrifices Shall Not Be Forgotten.

The names of those Aggies who gave their lives for their country are inscribed on the memorial plaque and in the hearts of their fellow students.

*"Postwar reconstruction ... was not a matter
of four or five years at A&M. It was nearly
twenty years before the College fully reestablished
its goals in tune with the times."*

Gibb Gilchrist, president, *1944–48*; chancellor, *1948–53*.
Courtesy Texas A&M University Archives.

X.

Proud and Painful Growth

Reconstruction and realignment—and near rebellion—typified the postwar world of Texas A&M. The war brought great changes in American technology and education, and A&M, along with most of the nation's institutions of higher learning, was still living by the guidelines established in the 1920s and 1930s.

A&M had been tremendously successful in wartime, and it was inconceivable that the College might face failure in peace. Pride, tradition, an outstanding war record, and a false sense of security created a greater resistance to change at A&M than at most institutions. Postwar reconstruction, then, was not a matter of four or five years at A&M. It was nearly twenty years before the College fully reestablished its goals in tune with the times.

After World War II, the Corps of Cadets and returning veterans seemed caught between the future and the past. Customs such as yell practice, muster, the bonfire, and observance of memorials took on the mantle of sacred rituals. An attack on hazing by the administration created a profound reaction among cadets. They believed what they were doing was right. Former students agreed. And when the administration successfully broke up hazing, it also broke the spirit of the Corps and created an atmosphere of gloom that enshrouded the entire College for a number of years.

The Corps, former students, faculty, and administrators were justifiably proud of A&M's war record.

Many asked why it was necessary to change a system that had proved itself in the past. Students revered A&M's war record simply by membership in the Corps. To be a cadet and to adhere to the traditions of the Corps was regarded as a form of patriotism and loyalty to school, country, and former students. This was especially true of young A&M students who had not participated in the war. They were proud of what had been accomplished. By association, they shared in those accomplishments. These same young men, though, were confused by the fact that the returning veterans they so greatly admired rejected the ritual, the hazing, and even the uniform they so respected themselves. It was a frustrating time for Aggies, both young and old.

The frustrations continued for many years. Change in any form was a threat to tradition. The idea of abolishing compulsory membership in the Corps of Cadets was greatly resented. There was the question of civilian students on campus. There were the questions of racial integration and coeducation. Even academic changes were viewed as an upheaval of the social order.

In 1942, a survey of the College conducted under the auspices of President Walton showed that Texas A&M required material improvement in basic research by its teachers, additional funds for the College library, an adequate student center, and additional space for classrooms, laboratories, and offices. A number of other improvements were called for.

A&M was, essentially, at odds with itself. In 1943–44 the board wanted to perpetuate the all-male military tradition of the College while at the same time renovating and modernizing the academic program. The Corps wanted to preserve tradition—if necessary, at the expense of modernization. On the other hand, some former students, faculty, and administrators wanted to modernize—if necessary, at the expense of tradition. All groups asked the question, could academic changes be made without altering long-established procedures and traditions?

President Walton appeared to have been caught on the horns of this Aggie dilemma. He announced in March, 1944, that his retirement from A&M had not been for reasons of ill health, but that he and the board had been in disagreement over matters of policy for the past three to five years. He believed, for example, the board placed too much emphasis on military training. After a special board meeting, directors announced that, while they basically agreed with Walton on the issues at stake, Walton's leadership had failed to keep pace with the College's growth, he had not supported the board's policies with "wholehearted compliance," and he had failed to exercise better control over the hazing situation.

The directors realized the need for fundamental academic changes but did not desire changes in A&M's military orientation. And, although there was no question that Texas A&M made great progress under Walton's administration, the College did appear to be falling behind academically. It seemed to be floundering without any clear objectives.

A Senate General Investigating Committee looked into the A&M situation. All sides in the controversy advised "doing what was best for A&M."

In May, 1944, the Texas A&M Board of Directors named Gibb Gilchrist to the presidency. Gilchrist, former head of the Texas Highway Department and dean of the School of Engineering at A&M, was a proven and successful administrator. He launched into his new job with his usual vigor and determination. He reorganized the academic and administrative structure of the College, upgraded many departments, created the Texas Research Foundation, and abolished the most serious forms of hazing. He became, on the one hand, one of the most admired and successful Texas A&M presidents and, on the other, one of the most disliked and controversial figures that ever appeared on the campus. He provoked a near revolution at Texas A&M without changing the basic character of the school as an all-male agricultural and engineering college with compulsory military training.

The appointment of Gibb Gilchrist as president marked the advent of Texas A&M's era of reconstruction. In 1943, the regular academic program had reached a virtual standstill because of lack of students. The board began to plan more carefully for the years ahead.

Gilchrist announced new academic goals. Essentially, there would be no revolution, but there would be greater efficiency. His first year in office was a relatively quiet and constructive one. War still raged overseas. The campus remained underpopulated.

A number of administrative changes took place. Between 1944 and 1947, over one-third of the academic departments acquired new heads. Numerous changes were made in the academic structure by combining or dividing older departments and creating new ones. Gilchrist inaugurated new plans for student administration and control; the old Discipline Committee was abolished and replaced by a faculty panel or jury. A director of student affairs assumed control over student life, completely relieving the commandant from such obligations.

One of the most important accomplishments of President Gilchrist's administration was the establishment of the Texas A&M Research Foundation. The foundation allowed industrial and private grants to be made to Texas A&M for research projects that would otherwise have been beyond the scope and legal authority of the College. Beginning projects included contracts dealing with the desalting of crude petroleum, studies in electric power transmission and distribution, and the location of hurricanes with radio direction finders. The program grew and by the 1960s was engaged in projects amounting to millions of dollars a year.

The most immediate and pressing problem facing Texas A&M and other schools and colleges across the nation after World War II was the "matter of instruction, feeding, housing and otherwise providing for" the returning veterans flocking back to campus under the G.I. Bill. Peacetime enrollment grew from the 1943–44 low of 2,000 to 8,651 for the 1946–47 year.

To house the increased number of students, dormitories were converted into married student apartments, and temporary family dwelling units were built. Trailers sprang up on the campus. Bryan Air Force Base was converted into dormitory and classroom spaces.

Because of the heavy enrollment of veterans, the

Corps Retreat, 1948. Courtesy Texas A&M University Archives.

General of the Army Dwight D. Eisenhower made his first stateside visit to Texas A&M on April 21, 1946. With Eisenhower are G. Rollie White ('95) and Gen. A. D. Bruce ('16). Courtesy Texas A&M University Archives.

board of directors discontinued the policy of requiring nonmilitary students to wear the uniform. With such a disparity in the student body, it was clear the military department, which regulated the Corps, could not be responsible for civilian students. Veterans would not accept the idea of a youngster in a uniform tell-

ing them what to do. New policies were adopted that better reflected the new student body and reasserted official control over student affairs.

In 1946, a dean of men was appointed to supervise student life. The professor of military science and tactics would exercise control and discipline only over the Corps. For the first time in its history Texas A&M recognized a civilian student body.

The directors were also aware that some of the old customs of the Corps could no longer apply to the postwar student body. Upperclassmen were prohibited from requiring students to perform services or run errands. No physical hazing was allowed, no extra drills. The new regulations, in the opinion of the Corps and many former students, struck at the heart of the Aggie traditions and the military regimen of the College.

When the new regulations were presented to the Corps, several students publicly tore them up. The entire Corps of Cadets marched on Gilchrist's home in protest. Over two hundred commissioned and noncommissioned officers submitted their resignations, stating they would not serve unless the regulations were repealed.

Gilchrist said little. What he did say left the cadets

Postwar enrollments found Texas A&M bursting at the seams. This 1947 registration was at the Annex, now called Riverside Campus. Fish or freshmen were housed and took classes at the Annex into the mid-1950s. Courtesy Texas A&M University Archives.

speechless: "I accept your resignations with regret." The protest march suddenly collapsed. Senior officers met after the march and voted to return to their units. They also presented a list of recommendations which essentially asked for reinstatement of most of Gilchrist's prohibitions. A few days later, a new list of demands was presented to College administrators. The demands included removal of Lt. Col. Bennie A. Zinn from all disciplinary control over the Corps, the removal of President Gilchrist, and the restoration of all cadet officer ranks. The authorities refused a mass reinstatement: each case would be individually considered. After three days of meetings, 143 cadet officers

accepted the school's ultimatum. The administration, and civilian control of the military establishment at Texas A&M, was unbowed and unbroken.

Public support for Gilchrist's stand against hazing poured in by mail, telegraph, and telephone. The board publicly endorsed his efforts. Said the *Dallas Morning News*, "Schoolboy soldiers who cannot grasp the first principle of soldiering have no right to run anything military—least of all the right to run A&M College."

By early February, fifty-seven cadet officers were reinstated. Eighty-seven others were returned to the ranks as privates. Peace seemed imminent. The Corps,

A&M President Gibb Gilchrist (left) and Governor Coke Stevenson at sunrise services, College Station, April 21, 1946. Courtesy Texas A&M University Archives.

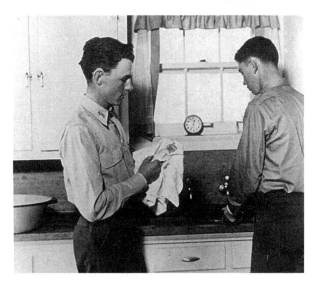

Two project house residents serve their time as dishwashers after a meal at one of the A&M College co-op project houses. Courtesy Texas A&M University Archives.

however, had not surrendered. Seniors resorted to written, notarized service contracts with freshmen. Col. Guy F. Meloy then banned the contracts.

Cadet representatives appeared before the board and criticized Gilchrist for the suppression of free speech. Cadet officers cast a vote of "no confidence" in two Corps officers.

Gloom and dissatisfaction spread to all parts of the campus.

Seniors, veterans, and other groups held meetings. Seniors and veterans asked for Gilchrist's dismissal. Veterans criticized the intimidation of faculty and students and charged that appropriations to the College were inadequate. While the protests of regular college students created little favorable response from Texans, a protest from veterans was something else. Their cries produced a state-wide response and an investigation from the House of Representatives. Accusations against Gilchrist mounted. The board defended the administration, stating it had ordered the president to eradicate hazing and that he was doing his job.

Gilchrist was clearly a man with vision and determination. His answers to questions raised by veterans were unequivocal and thwarted all charges of indiscretion or misuse of funds. The public and the legislature, however, felt that where there was smoke, there was bound to be fire. The Senate launched a joint legislative investigation. The board began a series of military trials of students charged with "disobedience of orders, insubordination and flagrant disregard of constituted authority."

The legislative investigation began. With few exceptions, board members, faculty, and administrators who testified strongly supported President Gilchrist. While Gilchrist was essentially exonerated, he and his administration were reprimanded for failure to command the full respect to which they should be entitled. Legislators added that this in no way should reflect upon the "successful administrative abilities of the president in other fields of endeavor." The cessation of the hearings brought a return of "domestic tranquility."

Veterans, however, asserted that political expediency had dictated the findings of the investigating committee. The Battalion published an editorial proposing that A&M cease being a military school and become a "civilian ROTC College." Its editor was given the "drown-out" treatment—inundated with buckets of water while in his room—by irate cadets.

Meanwhile, other things moved forward. Plans for a student union building were initiated. A number of faculty changes were announced. And the College adopted an official seal in September of 1947, choosing an unofficial seal which had long been in use.

The board's real response to the investigating committee's findings came in May, 1948. They created the Texas A&M College System, to be administered by a chancellor. Each component of the system would have an executive officer in charge designated by the president.

Gibb Gilchrist was named chancellor; David W. Williams, vice chancellor for agriculture; Frank C.

This view of the Corps of Cadets was taken for a Life magazine story on February 12, 1949. Courtesy Texas A&M University Archives.

The Ross Volunteers in 1950. Courtesy Texas A&M University Archives.

IN MEMORY OF STUDENTS OFFICERS AND FACULTY
OF
THE AGRICULTURAL AND MECHANICAL COLLEGE OF TEXAS
WHO VOLUNTEERED TO SERVE
THE UNITED STATES OF AMERICA
IN THE
SPANISH AMERICAN WAR 1898 – 1902
CUBA PUERTO RICO PHILIPPINES CHINA
ERECTED BY
AMERICAN MEMORIAL ASSOCIATION INC
1953

Spanish American War memorial erected on the A&M campus in Spence Park in 1953. Photograph by Jerry C. Cooper.

Bolton, president of the A&M College; Eugene J. Howell, president of John Tarleton; Ernest H. Hereford, president of North Texas Agricultural College; Edward B. Evans, president of Prairie View Agricultural and Mechanical College; and Marion Thomas Harrington, acting dean of the College and dean of the School of Arts and Sciences. All appointments were effective September 1, 1948.

During the four years of Gibb Gilchrist's administration as president, there were great changes at the College. Yet, beneath the surface, things remained strangely unchanged. It was still an agricultural and mechanical college with a predominantly military and exclusively all-male orientation, but one which possessed new capabilities. Trials and tribulations—and even more profound changes—lay ahead.

*"Earl Rudder brought Texas A&M University to
new heights of achievement, excellence and prestige."*

—*Senator Ralph Yarborough*
Houston Chronicle, March 25, 1970

James Earl Rudder, president, *1959–70*.
Courtesy Texas A&M University Archives.

XI.

Challenge and Change

Between 1948 and 1958, Texas A&M confronted change without really changing. Compared with the depression years, the war years, and the years immediately following the war, this decade marked a time of relative tranquility. There was concern, though, for things to come. Clearly looming on the horizon were co-education, elective military training, and the advent of a regular civilian student body. There were the challenges of racial integration, a burgeoning program of research and graduate study, and the development of a broader university complex. There was concern, too, for change afoot across the land. For in this ten-year period, the face of America was being remade.

Thirty-nine million babies were born in that decade. The population increased by thirty million. Narrow roads gave way to superhighways. Television came into almost every home. There was chicken—packaged and frozen—for every pot. There were air conditioners, dishwashers, and electric gadgets defying description. The new age produced hi-fidelity, FM radio, filtered cigarettes, drive-ins, supermarkets—and a chilling cold war.

The euphoria of victory following the end of World War II gave way too soon to a new threat of desperate conflict. In June, 1948, Russia closed off U.S. and Allied access to Berlin, a city administratively divided among the Big Four (U.S., Great Britain, France, and the Soviet Union). The West responded to the Soviet threat by organizing the Berlin Airlift and NATO.

Shortly afterward, the Soviet Union announced the development of a nuclear bomb. The U.S. halted its demobilization and began a peacetime mobilization.

In 1949, America's wartime ally in the Pacific, the Republic of China, collapsed to a Communist takeover. Chiang Kai-shek fled with his Nationalist armies to Formosa. In 1950, Communist forces of North Korea (divided along the 38th parallel for Russian and U.S. administration after World War II) attacked the Republic of South Korea. President Harry S. Truman sent American forces to the defense of South Korea. Texas Aggies went back to war. Thousands served. Fifty-seven gave their lives in the defense of freedom. Despite the Korean cessation of hostilities in 1953, the war continued to absorb American military forces. Over the next three decades Texas A&M sent its men, and eventually its women, to the 38th parallel and throughout the world in a cold and sometimes hot war that never ended.

Life and the military seemed inseparable. For a time Texas A&M felt that its commitment to the Corps of Cadets and military training for an all-male student body was again validated. Despite the fact that the world seemed to be in great change and flux, Texas A&M seemed somehow unchanged. But a quiet revolution was underway. In the 1950s and 1960s, the United States began what would become a technological and social revolution. These would not be easy times for academia, or for Texas Aggies, but they would

Faces change—and so do some aspects of student life. Courtesy Texas A&M University Photographic Services.

be exciting and challenging. Aggie professors and administrators such as Marion Thomas Harrington, who
served as president or as chancellor of Texas A&M
during most of the two decades, felt that somehow
"the faster we went, the behinder we got." One of
the first responses to change was to organize the Texas
A&M University System.

The creation of the Texas A&M College System in
1948 brought Gibb Gilchrist to the chancellor's chair
and Frank C. ("Bear Tracks") Bolton to the presidency
of the College. Bolton, inaugurated in November of
1948, had at that time completed almost forty years of
service at Texas A&M. He joined the faculty in 1909 as
the first head of the new Department of Electrical
Engineering, became dean of engineering in 1922,

*Frank Cleveland Bolton, acting president, 1943–44; president, 1948–50.
Courtesy Texas A&M University Archives.*

Aggies at Fort Hood, Texas, 1950. Many Aggies in the National Guard, Army Reserve, and regular service served their country during the Korean conflict. More than fifty died in combat. Courtesy Texas A&M University Archives.

A proud relic of A&M's past—the steam engine built by Frederick Ernst Giesecke and his classmates in 1886 as a senior engineering project. Giesecke joined the faculty in that year, and except for a fifteen-year period, remained at A&M until his retirement in 1945. Courtesy Texas A&M University Archives.

dean of the College in 1931, and served as acting president in the interim between Thomas Walton's administration and the election of Gibb Gilchrist to the presidency in 1944. He was a man for whom faculty, former students, and other associates held deep respect and admiration.

Many of the political chores and political storms were lifted from the president's shoulders by the presence of the chancellor, Gibb Gilchrist. Bolton and his successors, until 1965, could focus more attention on the academic and administrative affairs of the main college.

The system offered distinct advantages to the president of A&M, as well as to the presidents of branch colleges and directors of the services. The chancellor was in theory a systems man and not a Texas A&M College man. In practice, Texas A&M College continued to be the parent institution, not the peer of its branches. In theory, the chancellor held the reins on the powers of the president.

But there was a fallacy in the system: while Texas A&M College was bigger, more important, and more expensive than all of the other branches and services combined, it was administered by an official technically subservient to the chancellor. And, with both offices located on the same campus, the problem was even more delicate and ticklish. It was a case of the tail trying to wag the dog. Chancellors Gilchrist (1948–53) and Marion Thomas Harrington (1953–65)

President Marion Thomas Harrington (left) and Judge John W. Goodwin, member of the first class at A&M, in 1950. To the right of Judge Goodwin are Charles McGill, freshman student, and Governor Allan Shivers. Courtesy Texas A&M University Archives.

Aggies proudly pass in review on A&M's 75th Anniversary Day, October 4, 1950. Courtesy Texas A&M University Archives.

General Eisenhower with the cadet colonel and members of the Corps, 1950. Courtesy Texas A&M University Archives.

President Harrington and General Eisenhower. Courtesy Texas A&M University Archives.

A&M celebrates its 75th anniversary with a picnic for twelve thousand. Courtesy Texas A&M University Archives.

managed to coordinate the system from the chancellor's post with considerable success, but by 1965 control over the system was returned to the office of the president.

Stability, rather than change, was also characteristic of student enrollment at Texas A&M during the decade. Enrollments averaged something less than seven thousand a year. Also characteristic of these years was a relative decline in enrollment in agricultural studies, general stability in engineering, and growth in the arts and sciences.

A subcommittee on historical perspective, working under the auspices of the Texas A&M Century Council in the early 1960s, concluded that Texas A&M was fast losing its standing relative to other institutions of higher learning in the state. They attributed this to a number of factors, including the fact that A&M no longer had a monopoly on its courses and had lost any "uniqueness" it might formerly have had. Vocational training and engineering and agricultural studies had been pre-empted by most other institutions. The subcommittee pointed out that the College was segregated as to gender. It concluded too that the unique insistence on compulsory military training and military organization of the student body was detrimental to the College's academic programs and growth. Curricula in all fields needed to be broadened.

To be sure, some progress was being made in broadening the curricula and in improving the quality of programs. Some work was being done in the areas of noncompulsory military training and coeducation. Much more was to come.

During Frank Bolton's presidency, the board initiated a new building program. In the decade between 1948 and 1958, total construction amounted to more than $15 million. Bolton's tenure, however, was in some respects a caretaker regime. Only nine months after he took office, the board named Marion Thomas Harrington to succeed him. Harrington, who had been acting dean of the College and dean of the School of Arts and Sciences since 1948, assumed the president's office in 1950. He held a strong executive role at A&M from 1948 until his retirement as chancellor in 1965.

Harrington, a good academician and a capable administrator, sponsored a number of important innovations and developments while dean and president of the College. He promoted the organization of a Department of Oceanography and Meteorology. He guided expansion of the library. His administration saw authorization of a bachelor's and master's degrees in business administration. Also, in 1950, Texas A&M began preparations to celebrate its seventy-fifth anniversary. That event took place on October 4, 1950, with ceremonies in Kyle Field featuring Governor Allan Shivers and other notables.

Harrington's formal inauguration took place on November 9 of that same year. Dwight D. Eisenhower, then president of Columbia University, was the inaugural speaker at Kyle Field ceremonies. Harrington recalls a memorable gesture made by the former five-star general during the Corps review on the morning of the inauguration:

> We drove up to the MSC, and the R.V. escort, and the Cadet Corps was lined up to go out. He saw that the cadets did not have overcoats . . . he took off his topcoat after having ridden in the car with the heater on, and handed it to his aide. I kept mine on, and said, "General Eisenhower, wouldn't you like to have your topcoat?" He said. "No, as long as the students do not have it on, I'll not wear one."

Texas A&M's experience with the freshman division housed at the Bryan Air Force "Annex" between 1946 and 1950 proved academically sound. It provided a basic orientation program for entering freshmen and helped them channel their interests into likely fields of endeavor. When A&M closed down its academic program at the Annex in 1950, both Harrington and the faculty favored a formal "basic division" program on the main campus, "for the purpose of providing more adequately for the special needs of the entering students by making possible closer supervision and better guidance during their initial college careers."

Basic division dormitories were separated from the upperclass Corps area, but all freshmen continued to be enrolled in ROTC. Entering freshmen could elect to enroll in a general curriculum or in a degree curriculum within the school of their choice. The division offered "precollege" work in summer sessions.

By the mid-sixties, however, the division had been absorbed by the Counseling and Testing Service. Basic division course offerings gradually disappeared. All that remained was a summer program, a freshman orientation week, and a library collection labeled the "Basic Collection"—a bleak reminder of a noble effort gone astray.

Expansion of the Research Foundation continued rapidly through the fifties. The board created the Texas Transportation Institute to "do highway research." The oceanography department obtained its first seagoing vessel. A storm laboratory was established. The Memorial Student Center was completed in 1950. The Richard Coke Building was dedicated in 1951.

Charles Clement French resigned as dean of the

David Morgan, president, 1953–56. Courtesy Texas A&M University Archives.

College in 1952 and was replaced by David Hitchens Morgan. He was dean of the College for one year, until Gilchrist retired as chancellor. As the *Battalion* reported, Gilchrist turned over the chancellorship to Harrington, Harrington turned over the presidency to Morgan, and John Paul Abbott, who had been dean of arts and sciences since 1949, became dean of the College.

Harrington lauded retiring Chancellor Gilchrist as "an outstanding administrator of the vast A&M System covering the entire state. He has provided the leadership responsible for establishing the efficient operation of the System."

Gilchrist, like Bolton before him, retired as chancellor emeritus. He remained a strong supporter of Texas A&M until his death in College Station in 1972.

David H. Morgan was something of an unknown quantity, but a man who held great promise. During his first year on the campus the student newspaper selected him as one of six outstanding members of the faculty. He worked well with student leaders and the Corps of Cadets. He was a man who would have a good idea today and would want to see it in operation tomorrow. He was an aggressive man who, perhaps, tried to work too fast within the rather unwieldy A&M framework.

He worked hard and conscientiously at his new job. He was vitally concerned about the quality of

A&M's curricula offerings and appointed a standing Curriculum Committee.

The years 1948–58 found the Graduate School and the School of Arts and Sciences in particularly critical stages of development. As late as 1948, A&M was unequivocally a school for the training of agriculturists and engineers, and little else. Between 1948 and 1958, the proportion of students enrolled in the School of Arts and Sciences and in the Graduate School rose rapidly in comparison with enrollment in agriculture and engineering.

By 1948, the College had awarded ten Ph.D. degrees and about a thousand master's degrees. By 1958, A&M had granted 254 Ph.D. degrees and approximately 3,000 master's degrees.

Compared with what would come in the sixties and seventies, this represented only a marginal effort. The College's earlier preoccupation with undergraduate studies in agriculture and engineering proved to be a handicap. Texas A&M turned to the Rockefeller Foundation, which agreed to provide financial grants to selected faculty members so they could earn the Ph.D. degree. Some thirty members of the A&M faculty earned their doctoral degrees through this program over a ten-year period.

The School of Arts and Sciences also experienced a period of slow development between 1948 and 1958, only to come alive in the sixties and seventies. In 1948, the School of Arts and Sciences contained fourteen departments offering courses from biology to religious education. Considerable expansion took place in the next ten years, and, despite A&M's continuing role of offering service courses to agriculture and engineering, a strong foundation was being laid in the School of Arts and Sciences.

The Battalion offered students a funnier look at the campus when James Hubert Earle ('55) joined the staff and displayed his talents in the form of cartoons. Earle explains the origin of Cadet Slouch.

The beginning of Cadet Slouch in Texas A&M's The Battalion may be the least interesting story of all.

As a senior student in September of 1953, I approached the editors, Jerry Bennett and Ed Holder, and asked if they would be interested in including an occasional cartoon drawn by me. I was a little surprised when they were agreeable to my offer, so a few cartoons were drawn, submitted, and published.

After a moderate degree of success with general cartoons, it seemed appropriate to develop an identifiable character that could be used in the lead role of the cartoon. After a few sketches, a character was developed and named Cadet Slouch. The first appearance of a cartoon in which Slouch was given his own identity was just prior to Thanksgiving in 1953. Cadet Slouch became a regular feature of the Battalion, appearing four times per week.

Slouch was accepted as the spokesman for the student body by pointing out the humor in current situations in which we were all involved as students. The cartoons did not have to be good, clever, or well-done; it was only necessary that they reflect the current mood of the student body. I was always surprised when a rapidly drawn (and corny cartoon) would be remembered by someone as their favorite.

Since I was an architectural student with long labs, a pole vaulter on the track team, and member of the boxing team, I never had the time to do as good of a job with Slouch as I had wanted. It was always a "slopped out" cartoon done just in time to meet a deadline.

And the deadlines did not stop until 1985, after more than five thousand cartoons. By this time the Battalion had five issues per week. I decided to take a break after thirty-three years of deadlines, with the intention to do more later. Who knows, maybe Slouch will return.

Earle, Cadet Slouch's creator, received his bachelor's degree in architecture, a master's degree and doctorate in education—all from Texas A&M University. In 1957, he joined the faculty of the department of civil engineering and has been a part of A&M since his fish days. Together, since 1953, Jim Earle and Cadet Slouch have kept a finger on the pulse and have contributed mightily to the hearts and minds of Texas Aggies.

While President Morgan generally maintained a good relationship with the student body, several problems developed. In 1953, the faculty Student Life Committee established an editorial board for the Battalion, arguing that the student editorial staff needed assistance and guidance. The Battalion staff said the administration was attempting to censor and muzzle the student newspaper because it had been somewhat critical of past administrations. The Battalion staff resigned en masse. Morgan, then dean of the College, appointed a committee to investigate the situation, and the affair was soon smoothed over to the appar-

ent satisfaction of both students and administration.

Soon after becoming president, Morgan appointed a special faculty committee to study the ROTC situation. The committee reported that enrollment was declining, that A&M had an unusually high attrition rate, and that compulsory military training was limiting enrollment and diminishing the College's effectiveness in developing engineers, agriculturists, veterinarians, business executives, and other educated citizens. The committee recommended instituting noncompulsory military training. Morgan decided the noncompulsory Corps was a good idea and with the approval of the board made it effective for the opening of the fall term in 1954.

The change met with general approval by faculty members and students, but some students, and especially former students, were unhappy and irritated.

A renewal of hazing and the growth of secret organizations such as the mysterious "TT's," or True Texans, were met in positive fashion. Morgan suspended a number of students for being TT members, but reinstated them after the organization was allegedly dissolved.

Morgan, and A&M administrators, did not go so far as to allow women to enter A&M during the regular academic term. Coeducation was a much more controversial issue than even noncompulsory military

training. On March 3, 1953, Senator William T. Moore, a 1940 A&M graduate, introduced a resolution in the Senate which called for the admission of women to A&M. Moore argued that A&M had stagnated since the war and had experienced a decline in enrollment, partially because of its refusal to become coeducational. With little deliberation, the Senate adopted the resolution by voice vote.

Aggie reaction was characterized by a deluge of phone calls, telegrams, and letters, and caused the surprised Senate to reconsider the vote and rescind the resolution. Moore remained resolute and predicted A&M would be coeducational within ten years. As it turned out, he was right.

In this climate, Morgan, who held more liberal views on coeducation, made no effort to change the all-male status of the College. He had already made more changes than most former students could easily swallow. Any tampering with the Corps or student life as it had been in the past prompted the disaffection of many former cadets and some members of the board. Morgan moved too fast. Moreover, he provoked the displeasure of the chancellor and of members of the board over entirely minor situations.

One of the real handicaps of being president of Texas A&M during the fifties was the physical presence of the chancellor on campus. Theoretically, the

The Memorial Student Center, shortly after its completion in *1951*. This building is dedicated to the Aggie war dead. Courtesy Texas A&M University Archives.

Bill Dorsey, head yell leader, leads the cheers on All College Night, September *17*, *1956*. Courtesy Texas A&M University Archives.

Aggie band trumpeters sound Silver Taps at muster in *1951*. Earlier that day the new Memorial Student Center was dedicated. Courtesy Texas A&M University Archives.

president and not the chancellor was in charge of campus affairs, but it was virtually impossible for the chancellor, housed on the same campus, not to have a direct voice in College affairs.

Because Morgan incurred the displeasure of former students, the board, and the chancellor, and perhaps because, although he was tremendously capable, he was an impatient man, his resignation was

David Willard Williams, acting president, 1956–57. Courtesy Texas A&M University Archives.

Marion Thomas Harrington, president, 1950–53; chancellor, 1953–65. Courtesy Texas A&M University Archives.

requested by the Board. Morgan left A&M at the end of December, 1956, to become director of Dow Chemical's educational program.

D. W. Williams became acting president, in addition to his duties as vice chancellor for agriculture, and served from December, 1956, to September, 1957. He was a likeable, forthright, vigorous administrator and a good organization man, who stayed in the middle of things. In 1957, nearing retirement age and uninterested in remaining president on either an acting or regular basis, Williams recommended that the president's job be combined with that of chancellor and turned over to Tom Harrington. The board approved his recommendation and named M. T. Harrington president and chancellor.

Tom Harrington held the dual office of president and chancellor for two more years. The "chancellor" designation was dropped during this period, and his office was officially known as "President of Texas A&M and the System." In 1959, partly at the instigation of Harrington, the board reinstated the separation of the chancellor's office and the office of president of Texas A&M. The board made Harrington chancellor and named Earl Rudder president of the College. Rudder, an Aggie with a B.S. in industrial education, a major general in the U.S. Army Reserve, a hero of World War II, and commissioner of the Texas State Land Office from 1955 to 1958 (during which time he "cleaned up" the Texas land scandals), was widely regarded as one of the most unlikely men for the post of an aca-

demic presidency. He was considered least likely to rock the A&M boat or to effect any changes in the College. Those who held this view could not have been more wrong. Rudder restructured, revitalized, and revolutionized the institution. He built a university where a college had been before, and he dispelled many of the anxieties built up between 1948 and 1958.

Rudder served with great distinction in World War II. After the war he lived a quiet but active life as rancher, businessman, and mayor of Brady, Texas. He served as a member of the Texas Board of Public Welfare and the State Democratic Executive Committee. In 1955, Governor Shivers appointed Rudder to fill the post of Texas land commissioner.

On February 1, 1958, Rudder assumed the duties of vice president of Texas A&M, a position which made him in actuality the chief administrator of the College. Although Harrington held the joint title of president of A&M College and president of the A&M System, Rudder was in fact to be the real "president" and Harrington the "chancellor," although the chancellor's post had disappeared in name.

Rudder's impressive accomplishments were evi-

The Battalion has played an active role in campus activities throughout the College's history. Courtesy University News Service.

Always a busy time—registration, spring semester, 1960. Courtesy Texas A&M University Archives.

dent in far-reaching changes made during his tenure. He gave every appearance of being an Aggie of the old school, with old school ties, loyalties, traditions, and basic conservatism. A university in the throes of change, many anticipated, would not be helped along the way by such a man as Earl Rudder.

David W. Williams, acting president until September of 1957, had directed a questionnaire to the faculty at the request of the board. One of the questions was, should military training be optional or compulsory? The Academic Council favored optional military training by a vote of 49-1. The board voted to restore compulsory military training in November of 1957.

The policy change, in the face of the faculty's overwhelming disapproval, was even more disconcerting because news of the change leaked out before it could be announced by the board. The news appeared in the *Battalion* and was subsequently picked up around the state.

The *Houston Chronicle* noted that coeducation was at the real heart of the controversy and stated that 90 percent of the cadets opposed coeducation and favored compulsory membership in the Corps. The *Bryan Eagle* said, "A&M cannot play an effective role when hampered by philosophies of 1876." It called upon the board to take the necessary steps and make plans to admit women. The *Battalion* supported coeducation as well as noncompulsory military training but obvi-

ously failed to reflect the opinion of most students.

Long-standing coeducation champions, including State Senator William T. Moore, now rushed into the fray. In late January, 1958, the *Bryan Eagle* announced that John M. Barron ('35) would file suit in behalf of two women for admission to Texas A&M. The *Dallas Morning News* said John Barron was "a stubby Texas A&M College Aggie . . . destined to go into his alma mater's academic history as either a George Washington or a Benedict Arnold—depending on how you feel about female Aggies . . ."

In March, after a two-day hearing, Judge William T. McDonald gave Mrs. Barbara Tittle and Mrs. Lena Bristol authority to enroll in A&M. Texas A&M appealed the case. The Circuit Court of Appeals in Waco reversed Judge McDonald's decision. Plaintiffs appealed to the State Supreme Court, which refused to review. Then Vice-President Rudder commented, "The decision is in keeping with the Board of Directors' desire—it is my job to run A&M as the board wants it to run."

In September, 1959, three residents of Bryan started the controversy all over again. They applied for admission but were advised that the school was not coeducational. Again, Barron filed suit. The furor over coeducation was regenerated. One "pro-coeducation" student was injured by an ammonia bomb. The editor of the *Battalion* was "busted" in rank for an editorial supporting the admission of women.

The *1961* bonfire celebration begins. *Courtesy Texas A&M University Archives.*

John O. Teague (*'59*), seventh from right, parachuted into enemy territory near North Vietnam in *1966* to live with a South Vietnamese guerilla band, direct U.S. Air support missions, and provide rescue for downed U.S. pilots. *Courtesy Texas A&M University Archives.*

Judge McDonald, pointing to the higher court's reversal of the previous case, this time ruled against the admission of women. The U.S. Supreme Court refused to reconsider the decision of the lower courts. Texas A&M was still an all-male institution with compulsory military training, but, reported the *Battalion* years later, the suits "brought the problem out into the open."

Rudder was formally inaugurated president of A&M on March 26, 1960. He faced the difficult task of binding the wounds and quieting the tumult raised over the past two years, while steering A&M ahead in its academic development.

The year 1961 marked the eighty-fifth anniversary of the founding of Texas A&M. The recent past had been disturbing. The future was full of promise but brimming with uncertainties. It was clearly time for Texas A&M to do some soul-searching and self-evaluation. The board authorized a long-range planning study of the College.

Four independent studies of the College were conducted: the Faculty-Staff-Student Study on Aspirations; Report of the Century Council; Report to Commission on Colleges, Southern Association of Colleges and Schools; and the report which capped these vari-

ous efforts, the Board of Directors' Blueprint for Progress.

While the various study groups devoted thousands of man-hours and thousands of pages of written material to evaluating the school, the final reports comprised a total of about six hundred pages. They contained both specific and broad statements as to where A&M had been and where it planned to go. Recommendations included:

1. Changing the name of the institution to foster and maintain a university image.

2. Establishing a tenure policy in conformity with national standards.

3. Recognizing outstanding teaching and research.

4. Bringing an end to compulsory military training and the all-male admissions policy.

5. Establishing higher admission standards.

6. Initiating a $55 million building program [which eventually grew to almost $155 million] to be completed by 1976.

7. Construction of an oceanography and meteorology building.

8. Acquisition of a cyclotron accelerator.

Although broad in its context, the meaning, purposes, and importance of the Board's Blueprint for Progress, adopted in 1962, cannot be overestimated in their significance to the developing university over the next fourteen years. The Blueprint included the following objectives:

1. The College shall stress systematic and selective program development.

2. The College shall place increasing emphasis upon the development of strong interdisciplinary programs in the areas of engineering and the sciences.

3. The College shall encourage and facilitate the continuing and increasing use of the most modern teaching devices and techniques in College programs.

The various self-study reports not only reflect that the times of post-war reconstruction and the anxieties of 1948–58 were over, but that Texas A&M had been aroused and awakened to new efforts. Within a year after completion of the reports, two important changes occurred at Texas A&M. The College became coeducational, with some restrictions, and Texas A&M became Texas A&M University. The board agreed to admit women on a limited basis; that is, in addition to the "normal requirements" for admission, a woman had to be the wife or daughter of an enrolled student or faculty or staff member. The action caught most Aggies by surprise.

Board President Sterling C. Evans said that the board had no plans to make A&M an "all-out coed institution." Rudder called a meeting of the entire Corps of Cadets. He was greeted with boos and hisses by angry cadets who chanted, "We don't want to integrate." At A&M integration referred to females—not blacks.

Rudder appealed to the cadets' school spirit. The Corps accepted his statement, but they never did like it. Some students, in shocked disbelief, said it was like West Point going coed. Others reflected pleasant surprise. One group of cadets formed the Committee for an All Male Military Texas A&M. "We will carry this issue to the people of Texas," they declared.

Reactions from the public and former students were mixed. "One thing for sure," a newspaper reporter observed, "No Aggie is indifferent. An indifferent Aggie is about as rare as a dodo bird. Aggies just aren't made that way."

A random questioning of Abilene "exes" brought such comments as "Big mistake!" "Next, they'll abolish the Corps of Cadets." "I'm 54 years old and I still like girls—but not at A&M." "It's about time they had some coeds there and started having a little fun."

On May 7, 1963, State Representative Will Smith sought to introduce a bill before the legislature requiring Texas A&M to remain all-male. He failed to get the necessary vote for introduction but did succeed in getting the House to approve a resolution requiring the state to maintain one major university for men and one for women. Over five hundred Aggies turned out to support the resolution. The resolution passed. Senator William Moore sought to balance the scales by gaining Senate approval of a resolution supporting A&M's coeducational decision. There the matter rested until the next session of the legislature, when yet another spirited fight developed.

Twelve women applied for admission to A&M within two days after the policy change was announced. By September, 1963, 150 women were enrolled at A&M. Women could come, but for the most part they were not made welcome. Few buildings had rest rooms for women. No dormitories were opened for women until the fall of 1972. But change was clearly in the air.

In 1965, the board authorized Rudder to use his "discretion" in admitting women. More applications were approved. By September, 1971, all pretenses were abolished by the board, and women were to be admitted on an equal basis with men. The *Catalog* read, "Texas A&M University is a coeducational university admitting all qualified men and women to all academic studies on the same basis without regard to race, creed, color or national origin."

And it was truly so. By 1974, 25 percent of the student body were women. After almost one hundred years, one of the major disputes and most vexatious issues had been settled. Had Texas A&M lost that certain something that made it distinctive? Many Aggies thought so.

Many also felt they were being buffeted severely by the winds of change. Effective August 23, 1963, the legislature approved a bill changing the name of the Agricultural and Mechanical College of Texas to Texas A&M University. Under the new designation the

Female cadets become a part of the oldest tradition at Texas A&M—the Corps of Cadets. Courtesy Texas A&M University Photographic Services.

"A&M" simply retained the old, familiar sound—it did not mean Texas Agricultural and Mechanical University. But the old, familiar sound was not enough to suit many Aggies. They wanted the old, familiar name back, too.

Wrote Jack Gallagher for the *Houston Post*, "When they start tampering with the good name of Texas A&M, well, they've overstepped their bounds. . . . Those curriculum-broadeners went to work and changed Texas A&M College to Texas A&M University. What comes out now is as flat as the Brazos bottoms."

The board announced yet another change in November, 1964. Chancellor Harrington would retire. James Earl Rudder would become president of Texas A&M University and president of the Texas A&M University System. Said Rudder, "Texas A&M is greatly indebted to Dr. Harrington for his contributions. . . . I am pleased to follow in the steps of this great man."

Harrington, after fifty years of service as a student, teacher, and administrator, proudly continued to serve his school as coordinator of the international programs until 1971, when he was named president emeritus. His is a great example of the strong dedication and able service that so many Aggies have given their alma mater.

Rudder, a dedicated Aggie with unbounded energy and determination, knew no rest. Three new

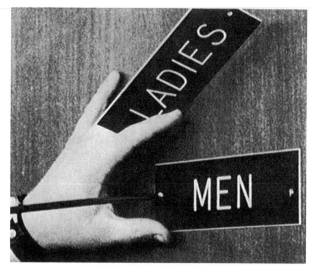

The end of one era and the beginning of another, as coeducation comes to A&M at the end of the first century. Courtesy Texas A&M University Archives.

colleges and deans were established: the Graduate College, now under Dean George W. Kunze; the College of Geosciences, now headed by Earl F. Cook; and the College of Science, now under Dean John M. Prescott. By 1968, Texas A&M had attained university status, increased its enrollment to almost double that of ten years before, expanded its research program monu-

Alvin Roubal Luedecke ('32), acting president, March to October, 1970, is presently executive vice-president of the University. Courtesy Texas A&M University Archives.

mentally, broadened the curriculum, upgraded academic and faculty standards, and initiated a multimillion dollar building program.

The $6 million cyclotron complex was a reality. The Olin E. Teague Research Center was completed. The library was expanded with a four-story, modern addition. The College of Business Administration was established under the direction of Dean John Earle Pearson. To top it all, Texas A&M won the 1967 Southwest Conference championship in football and the Cotton Bowl game on New Year's Day, 1968.

Without fanfare, notice, or disturbance, atypical of the pattern through the South and Southwest in the 1960s, Texas A&M also became racially integrated.

In 1970, the School of Education separated from the College of Liberal Arts to become the College of Education, headed by Dean Frank W. R. Hubert. W. David Maxwell became dean of liberal arts. By 1971, the old war school had a dean of women, Toby Rives. Anything, seemingly, could happen at Texas A&M.

At a time when many college campuses, notably San Francisco State and Kent State, were experiencing the shock of campus turmoil and rioting, Texas A&M felt only minimal unrest. Rudder promised a "hell of a fight" to any would-be troublemakers at Aggieland. He was quite outspoken against the rising trend to unkempt dress and hair styles sweeping the country. "A prof who wears a beard in the classroom is just trying to substitute a beard for knowledge," he said. Even in that respect, A&M was changing. Long hair, pork-chop sideburns, beards, "hot pants," and bare feet became evident on the campus. The cadets in the Corps, however, maintained their traditional, neat, well-groomed appearance.

The University continued to build. The $10 million Zachry Engineering Center was completed in 1972. A $10 million auditorium and continuing education and conference tower complex began to rise on the campus and was completed in 1973. Easterwood Airport was upgraded with instrument landing facilities and extended runways. A new $8.5 million dormitory complex named for C. C. Krueger ('12) and J. Harold Dunn ('25) was completed in 1972.

Earl Rudder was constantly in the middle of all activities. He was tough but fair. He never spared himself. He brought A&M to new heights of achievement. In late January, Rudder became ill and was rushed to a local hospital. Later, he was transferred to a Houston hospital. He underwent brain surgery and died in Houston on March 23, 1970.

Rudder lay in state on the morning of March 25 in the rotunda of the System Administration Building. Former President of the United States Lyndon Johnson and members of Rudder's old Ranger command were among the thousands on hand to pay tribute.

Rudder was one of the truly great Aggies in both peace and war. Said the *San Angelo Times*, "He served his state and his nation throughout his life; that his life has now ended means we have all suffered the loss of a distinguished and dedicated friend . . ."

After Rudder's death, the board named Maj. Gen. Alvin Roubal Luedecke ('32) acting president of the University while the search began for "the most qualified person in the United States" to fill the presidency on a permanent basis. W. Clyde Freeman, vice president and comptroller, Horace R. Byers, vice president for academic affairs, and Tom D. Cherry, vice president for business affairs, provided leadership in the interim.

Luedecke was quietly efficient as the ad interim

Returning Vietnam POW Captain James E. Ray ('63) is met by his mother in San Antonio. Courtesy Associated Press.

Aggie Maj. Al Meyer ('60), returning POW, is greeted by his wife at Kelly Air Force Base. Courtesy Texas A&M University Archives.

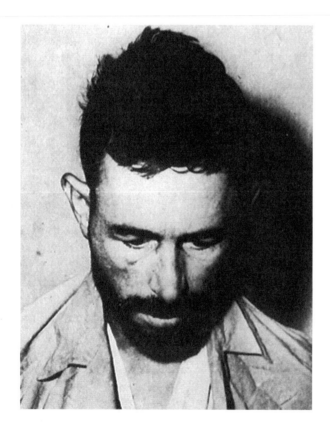

Maj. Robert Norlan Daughtrey ('55) during his captivity in North Vietnam. Courtesy Texas A&M University Archives.

Major Daughtrey is greeted by his family after his return from a POW camp in North Vietnam. Courtesy Texas A&M University Archives.

Commencement, *1973*. Courtesy Texas A&M University Archives.

Aggies, *"all for one, and one for all!"* Courtesy Texas A&M University Photographic Services.

administrator of the University. One of his accomplishments was to remove the final restrictions regarding the admission of women. Although Rudder had for the past year or two maintained an open-door policy for women, the "daughter-wife" restriction remained in the book. Beginning in September, 1971, A&M became fully coeducational by profession, as it had been for several years in practice.

The Rudder years were years when the reconstruction of the old College was finished and the construction of the new University began. James Earl Rudder had brought together the many fine programs begun since World War II and helped form those elements into a compound with the older institutions and traditions to create a more cohesive, integrated University.

A nice day in Aggieland. A fountain-side view of Harrington Education Center and Annex. Courtesy Texas A&M University Photographic Services.

The final resting place for the fightin' Texas Aggie mascots is at the entrance to Kyle Field so they can see the scoreboard. Courtesy Texas A&M University Archives.

The Civil Engineering/Texas Transportation Institute Building, completed in 1987. Courtesy Texas A&M University Photographic Services.

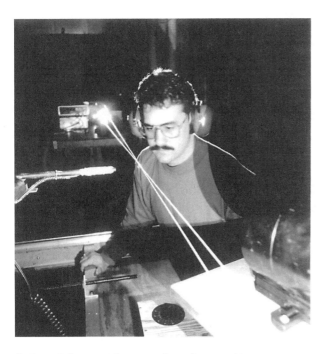

Ammon Underwood ('o7), for whom Underwood Hall is named, endowed four A&M President's Scholarships, gave the University valuable real estate, and then willed his estate to Texas A&M. Courtesy Texas A&M University Photographic Services.

"What will the twenty-first century bring?" Courtesy Texas A&M University Photographic Services.

All Faiths Chapel. Courtesy Texas A&M University Archives.

*"Grave responsibilities rest upon you.
The excellence of the college will be
determined by your progress."*

Nearly fifty years of alumni directors. Left to right: Executive Directors of the Association of Former Students Dick Hervey ('42), *1947–64*;
E.E. McQuillan ('20), *1927–47*; Richard ("Buck") Weirus ('42), *1964* through the present. Photo by Jerry C. Cooper.

XII.

Into the Second Century

It was one of those nice, cool, crisp mid-October Texas evenings. The sweltering heat of September finally had faded from memory. Thomas Gathright, his five professors, their families, and the first six students of the just-opened Agricultural and Mechanical College of Texas felt good that the first week of school was behind them. And they felt good about the supper, just finished. Plenty of good Texas beef and fresh baked bread and honey. Cadet Martin Durkin offered a satisfied sigh, left the table, and walked up the short flight of stairs, out the front door of Gathright Hall to stand on the doorstoop. He was suddenly hit and knocked to the floor by a ball of furry fury, followed by a host of growling beasts. "I'm killed! I'm killed!" he hollered.

Cadets and adults piled up the stairs to the front stoop to see what was happening. When they threw open the doors, wolves lurched away growling and moaning into the brambles and prairie grasses surrounding the building. Cadets grabbed Martin, dragged him into the building, and slammed the doors.

Downstairs, Julia Banks, the wife of mathematics professor Alexander Banks, stared in disbelief out the ground-level casement windows. Wolves scratched and clawed on the window panes as if anxious to get in and join the feast below.

Their drooling mouths and blood shot eyes were a horrifying sight. Mrs. Banks wondered why she and her husband had ever come to this dreadful place.

One hundred years later some students and faculty may still have been asking themselves that same question. But for each one of those there were now tens of thousands of students, former students, and faculty who knew the answer. They had come to Texas A&M University to get or to help give an education, to participate in the Aggie experience, and to imbibe of the Aggie spirit.

Texas A&M emerged from World War II more strong, more proud, and more assured of its past, its present, and its purposes. For almost a quarter of a century Texas A&M confronted change—without really changing. But that too changed. Now, in the last quarter of the twentieth century, Texas A&M evolved and expanded to meet the changing and diverse needs of the state, the nation, and the rising global community. The evolution of Texas' oldest public university into a world-class university often met resistance—both inside and outside the community. Change was difficult at Texas A&M. It was not a revolutionary process. Change always evoked challenge. It did not always bring progress. But throughout those changes Aggies preserved a commonality of experience, a Texas Aggie experience, that made Texas A&M not only a great but a unique and distinctive institution.

Change, in part, involved physical growth. Much of that growth occurred in the last decade of the school's first century and in the first decade of its second century. After 1976, enrollment grew by an average of one thousand students each year. Not only did enrollments grow, but the composition and quality of students changed. Ninety-nine percent of the Aggies came from the top academic half of their high schools, and more than 50 percent graduated in the top quarter of their high school classes. By 1990, Texas A&M enrolled over forty thousand students—one-fifth of them graduate students, almost half of them women, and many of them African-American, Hispanic, Asian, Native American, and foreign students. This enrollment reflected the diversity of American life, the national

171

The Dallas A&M Mothers' Club of *1926*. This club, organized by Mrs. H. L. Peoples (fourth from left) in *1922*, encouraged formation of other clubs in Fort Worth, Brownwood, San Antonio, Bell County, Brazos County, Houston, and San Angelo. In *1928* these clubs joined in forming the Federation of Texas A&M Mothers' Clubs. Courtesy Texas A&M University Archives.

prominence of the University, and its rising position among world academic institutions.

Texas A&M achieved a position as one of the top twenty universities in research expenditures and as one of the top ten in enrollment of merit scholars. Texas A&M's Colleges of Veterinary Medicine and Engineering had the largest enrollments of any in the nation. The College of Business, organized in the late sixties, grew into one of the major academic sectors of the University, at both the graduate and undergraduate levels, and gave A&M a business profile that complemented the traditionally strong agricultural, engineering, and science components. The College of Medicine, authorized by the Texas Legislature in 1971, enrolled its first class of thirty-two students in 1977, awarded the first M.D. degrees in 1981, and joined the ranks as one of Texas' major fully-accredited medical schools by the nineties. Not coincidentally, Bryan and College Station concurrently developed major commercial medical complexes.

In most years Texas A&M led other colleges and universities in annual giving by its alumni—the vaunted Association of Former Students. The Association of Former Students, in cooperation with the De-

The Alumni Administration Award, the Alumni Giving Award, and the Alumni Service Award—three outstanding awards given to the Texas A&M University Association of Former Students by the American Alumni Council. Courtesy Texas A&M University Archives.

velopment Foundation, provided funding for a growing array of alumni professorships and presidential scholars for faculty teaching and research awards and for faculty development leaves.

Located on the west campus, the Herman F. Heep and Minnie Belle Heep Building houses Texas A&M's soil and crop science programs. Photograph by James Lyle. Courtesy Texas A&M University Photographic Services.

The fields and farms west of the campus became home to the College of Medicine, an enlarged veterinary medical campus, a research center, and the new College of Agriculture complex. New buildings included the Kleberg Animal and Food Sciences Center, named for Robert Justus Kleberg, Jr.; the Heep Center for Soil and Crop Sciences named for Minnie Belle and Herman F. Heep ('20); the Rosenthal Meat Science and Technology Center named for distinguished alumnus E. M. "Manny" Rosenthal ('42); a five-story biochemistry/biophysics building; the Horticulture and Forest Science Building; the Reynolds Medical Sciences Building and the Medical Sciences Library, named for Houston attorney and former Regent Joe H. Reynolds; and a greatly expanded veterinary medical complex that included a new clinical sciences building completed in 1989. Growth, in part, was very physical and was by no means confined to the new west campus.

The "old" campus, modernized and landscaped before 1976, almost doubled again in classroom, office, and dormitory space in the next score of years. Somewhat like the eye of an inverted needle, Albritton

Bell Tower, donated by Martha and Ford D. Albritton ('43) and located at the old West Gate near the railroad track, sews together the old and new campuses. The carillon bells ring: "With pride and honor for all past, present and future students of Texas A&M University." Some distance away the new former students embassy, the Clayton W. Williams, Jr., Alumni Center, helps preserve the spirit of 150,000-plus living Aggie former students.

In the northeast quadrant of the campus, new engineering classroom and office buildings overshadow the still-new Zachry Engineering Building. An eight-story aerospace engineering and computer science building house state-of-the-art laboratories for teaching cognitive systems visualization, discrete computation, robotics, real-time systems, and artificial intelligence. Completed in 1983, the Wisenbaker Engineering and Research Center, named for Regent Royce E. Wisenbaker ('39), houses administrative offices and laboratories. The ten-story Joe C. Richardson, Jr. ('49) Petroleum Engineering Building, completed in 1989, reaffirms the prominence of petroleum in Texas commerce and education. A new wing of old

The Michel T. Halbouty Geosciences Building. Photograph by Michael Kellett. Courtesy Texas A&M University Photographic Services.

Geology-Petroleum Building dwarfs the old and bears a new name for the whole—the Michel T. Halbouty ('30) Geosciences Building, while an eight-floor civil engineering and transportation institute building, completed in 1987, contains laboratories, offices, classrooms, and the Pie Are Square cafe.

As if that weren't enough, many of the old buildings on campus were renovated and recast for new roles. The old Easterwood Terminal gave way to the McKenzie Terminal, serviced by four major airlines. The systems building, standing as a sentinel at the East Gate, conceded its systems administrative offices to a new munificent off-campus building named for former Texas Governor John B. Connally.

Not least, the University library obtained its one millionth volume in 1976, and within the next quarter of a century almost again doubled its holdings. Change seemed the order of the day as A&M marched bravely into its second century. But there seemed to be disproportionately more stress and strain in the changing order of things. Enrollment in the Corps of

The Royce E. Wisenbaker Engineering and Research Center, named for A&M regent and distinguished alumnus. Courtesy Texas A&M University Photographic Services.

William A. McKenzie Terminal. Courtesy Texas A&M University Photographic Services.

The Sterling C. Evans Library is the academic heart and information center of the campus. Photograph by Michael Kellett. Courtesy Texas A&M University Photographic Services.

Cadets, the keepers of tradition and the caretakers of the Aggie spirit, declined precipitously, sometimes falling below two thousand or only 5 percent of the total student body. Not too many years earlier, almost all Texas A&M students had been male, and almost all were members of the Corps of Cadets. Following the admission of women into the Corps of Cadets in 1974, women eventually comprised 5 percent of the Corps of Cadets. Even the Aggie Band, a traditional all-male bastion, became "integrated"—meaning women became band members.

Fraternities and sororities began to appear. One fraternity member said in 1976, "They know we're here, but they act as if they don't." The University first declined to extend official recognition to fraternities and sororities. Virtually nonexistent before 1976, they became prominent in student affairs in the 1980s. The University recognized fraternities in 1985 and sororities in 1990.

Students, former students, and faculty clashed variously over many issues facing the University: whether "frats" should be allowed; if students should walk on the grass or build bonfire; if women in the Corps could be "qualified" to wear senior boots; if bonfire should be moved to another location; if

Assault on a fire—an exercise in modern, specialized fire-fighting at A&M. The annual Fireman's Training School is one of the many programs conducted by the Engineering Extension Service which help make Texas cities and towns better places to live. Courtesy Texas A&M University Archives.

women should be admitted to the Aggie Band; if sororities and fraternities were basically subversive of the Aggie Spirit; if a homosexual student organization should be recognized; and if seniors should be required to take final examinations. The scene was divisive, the tumult jarring, and the prospects of resolution distant. The truth was that a lot of the sound and fury of the seventies and eighties signified much less than appearances argued.

The real substantive decisions for change were now historic and well-established. The initiatives taken by the architect of change, Gen. James Earl Rudder, established the blueprint for the reconstruction and redirection of the old Agricultural and Mechanical College. By 1976, at the close of its one hundredth year of operation, Texas A&M had already achieved a fundamental transition, but that transition only now became truly recognizable in the dawning of its second century. For the first one hundred years Texas A&M was, despite changes, an all-male, Texas-oriented, largely undergraduate instructional institution with a focus primarily in engineering, agriculture, and the military. The advent of the second hundred years

The Fightin' Texas Aggie Band displays their spirit. Courtesy Texas A&M University Photographic Services.

The Olin E. Teague Research Center. Research is a vital arm of A&M's threefold approach to higher education: teaching, research, and extension. Courtesy Texas A&M University Archives.

marked its emergence as a very different institution, while it somehow preserved the essence of the old.

While the old conservatism and caution provided something of a protective umbrella, new ideas and "a liberation of thought" emerged. A greater diversity existed, but a pervasive sense of Aggies still comprised the traditional "one great fraternity." The Corps of Cadets and military training became but a small segment in the Aggie tapestry but somehow continued to set the tone of the whole. There was discord over race, minorities, sexual harassment, political correctness, multiculturalism, and homosexuality, but a widespread sense that "We Are (nonetheless) the Aggies!" One still walked the campus feeling propelled by a sea of "howdies." New age former students, judging by their giving, their caring, and their participation, "bled maroon" no less than those of another time. Despite the growth and the greater focus on graduate studies and research, Texas A&M boasted more "real" faculty than comparable institutions in that tenured

and tenure-track faculty did most of undergraduate teaching. As in the past, professors really were in the classroom.

The perception of what A&M had become seemed to lag behind the reality by several decades. The institution was not what even many "old Ags" perceived it to be and was far beyond the image considered by the outside world. That misconception fit in part with the prevailing myth that Texas was itself a lawless land of cactus, prairies, and cowboys, while the reality of petroleum and computer industries, medical complexes and space industries, international agribusinesses and urban sprawl were somehow lost in the romanticism of gone but not forgotten past. Just as the old A&M College led Texas' modernization into the railroad, automobile, and airplane age, so to had the new Texas A&M University become an incubus for the leap forward into the twenty-first century of "hi-tech," space, computers, global communications, agribusiness, and international commerce.

Of course, some things did not change at Texas A&M. Although it may sound contrived and artificial in an age of cynicism and sophistication, Aggies of the past and present shared an inordinate and unusual affection for their school that is inscribed in the almost indefinable "Aggie spirit," something that had survived very well into the second hundred years.

The Aggie Ring

Frank W. Cox, III gives a description of the Aggie ring, in I *Bleed Maroon* (1992) that provides good insight into the indomitable Aggie spirit:

> The ring serves as a common link for former students. When an Aggie sees a ring on another Aggie's hand, a spontaneous reunion occurs.
>
> The shield on the top of the ring symbolizes our desire to protect the good reputation of our school. The thirteen stripes in the shield refer to the thirteen original states and symbolize the intense patriotism of graduates of Texas A&M. The five stars in the shield refer to the five phases of development of the student: mind or intellect, body, spiritual attainment, emotional poise, and integrity of character. The eagle is symbolic of agility, power, and ability to reach great heights and ambitions.
>
> One side of the ring symbolizes the seal of the State of Texas. The five-pointed star is encircled with a wreath of olive leaves symbolizing achievement and a desire for peace. The live oak leaves symbolized the strength to fight. They are joined at the bottom by a circled ribbon to show the necessity of joining these two traits to accomplish one's ambitions to serve.
>
> The other side with its ancient cannon, sabre, and rifle symbolizes that Aggies are willing and determined to defend our homeland. The sabre stands for valor and confidence. The rifle and cannon are symbols of preparedness and defense. The crossed flags of the United States and Texas recognize the dual allegiance to nation and state. The gold represents purity and the sacrifices of our parents.

The traditions and values symbolized have provided a steadying course for Aggies and Texas A&M in times of almost frenetic change.

The Smell of Change

As the seventeenth president of Texas A&M University, Jack Kenny Williams warned in his inaugural address on April 16, 1971: "In matters large and small, the atmosphere of education is heavy with the smell of change. For some of us this is heady perfume; for others it is the pungent odor of brimstone." Williams explained that we must sail the seas of change with whatever navigational experience we have or can command, or we will become passengers on educational vessels manned by others.

A person uniquely suited to administer change while preserving tradition, Williams, named president of Texas A&M and of the Texas A&M University System on November 1, 1970, followed Gen. James Earl Rudder's death and the acting presidency of Gen. Alvin Roubal Luedecke. Governor Preston Smith described him as "an administrator who rises to the challenge of a complex and difficult task of space-age education but one who is also capable of preserving the traditions which have proved themselves to be valuable."

After rising to the rank of major in World War II, Williams went to Emory University where he earned a master's degree in 1947 and a doctorate in history in 1953. He began his teaching career at Clemson in 1947. He was named dean of the Clemson graduate school in 1957, dean of faculties in 1960, and vice president for academic affairs in 1963. He came to Texas in 1966 as the first commissioner of the Coordinating Board of the Texas College and University System, where he helped lay the groundwork for the development of current and long-range planning for the state's junior and senior colleges and universities. In 1968, he went to Tennessee as vice president for academic affairs for the six-campus University of Tennessee System and served in that capacity until his appointment as president of Texas A&M University and of the Texas A&M University System.

The winds of change, sometimes spring freshets and sometimes winter storms, blew vigorously across Aggieland. The winter storms sometimes swept the Aggies to the far reaches of the earth. The Vietnam War became a quagmire of military conflict and social conscience. Thousands of Texas Aggies went to Vietnam; many endured years as a prisoner of war. One hundred five—almost twice as many as in Korea—gave their lives in combat for their country. Unlike Korea, it seemed to be a war with no real beginning, but like Korea, it was a war that refused to end. And as the war progressed, or failed to progress, the smell of change became more pungent.

During the seven years of Williams's administration, A&M crossed the threshold from its first into its second century. Enrollments soared from 14,221 students in the fall of 1970 to more than 29,500 students

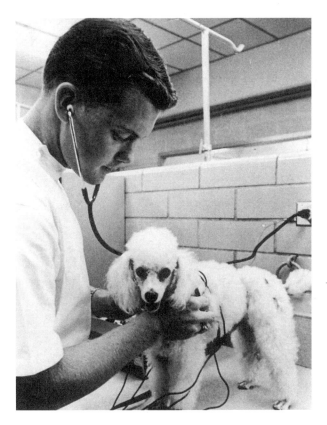

Interior of the Nuclear Science Center near Easterwood Airport. Courtesy Texas A&M University Archives.

Veterinary medicine has come a long way since the pioneering days of Dr. Mark Francis. Courtesy Texas A&M University Archives.

The nuclear reactor is a demonstration and learning tool for nuclear engineers. Courtesy Texas A&M University Archives.

in the fall of 1977. The *Battalion* said on August 30, 1977, that the campus was a "carpet of congestion." There was no place to park, and for many, no place to sleep. During registration several hundred students slept on makeshift beddings in hallways waiting for assignment to rooms that simply did not exist. The costs of room, board, and laundry began to rise. Classrooms overflowed. But for all this, excitement was in the air.

And an environment, history, and system for channelling the enormous energies and talents of tens of thousands of students existed. A new student affairs office managed to amalgamate traditions inherited from the Corps of Cadets and the Student "Y" (YMCA) Association activities with current programs of the Memorial Student Center and services provided by the office of the dean of students. A student-led society emerged which made the Texas A&M educational experience something truly unique and remarkable.

The prime mover in shaping the student-life environment for A&M's second century was John J. Koldus, III, whom President Jack Williams brought to the A&M campus as dean of students in 1973, replacing James P. Hannigan who retired. Formerly a teacher of history and civics at high schools in Arkansas and Amarillo and then a professor of psychology and vice president for student affairs at East Texas State University, Koldus sought "to make the learning experience of each and every student the best it can be."

In 1974, President Williams approved Koldus's plan to consolidate the offices of dean of men and dean of women under his direction as vice president of student services with the Memorial Student Center, Student Health Services, and Corps of Cadets as reporting but largely autonomous divisions. He created a student activities office under the direction of Carolyn Adair ('69), which counseled more than 150 student organizations and had oversight for the vocal music programs, such as the Singing Cadets. An off-campus housing and support office extended student services and support to fully two-thirds of the student population who lived in community apartment complexes. A student legal services office, multi-cultural services office, handicapped student services office, "Fish Camp" for new students, and "T" Camp for transfer students provided a helping hand to young Aggies.

The result was a strengthening of the Aggie bond, an enriched educational experience, and, despite the trauma of growth and the stresses of a teeming social environment, an unusually mature, motivated, and re-

Jack Kenny Williams became president of A&M in 1970. Courtesy Texas A&M University Archives.

sourceful student who, as in the past, was a rather unique being—the Texas Aggie.

To be sure the burdens and challenges of growth were truly wearing, particularly on many faculty and administrators. Following a heart attack in 1976, the regents decided to give President Jack Kenny Williams some relief from the dual responsibilities of administering both Texas A&M University and its affiliated institutions and agencies, each experiencing the trauma of growth, and often their own special set of problems. The regents reinstated the chancellorship that had been dormant for the past twelve years.

On May 24, 1977, Jack Williams became chancellor of the Texas A&M University System and acting president of Texas A&M University until a president could be selected. Chairman of the Board of Regents H. G. "Clyde" Wells said, "The job is too large for any one person."

Change: Conflict and Consensus

After an extensive national search for a new president, the board of regents found one at home. On August 1, 1977, Dr. Jarvis E. Miller ('50), director of the Texas Agricultural Experiment Station, became

Even in the early days, Aggies had their eyes on tomorrow ... but the tomorrows we envision always fall far short of reality ... and that's as it should be ...

The equestrian statue adjoining the Kleberg Animal and Food Science Center is Robert Justus Kleberg, Jr., owner and director of the world-famous King Ranch from *1935* until his death in *1974*. He received an honorary degree in agriculture from Texas A&M in *1941* for his contributions to Texas' cattle and livestock industry and for his support of Texas A&M. Photograph by James Lyle. Courtesy Texas A&M University Photographic Services.

The Clayton W. Williams, Jr., Alumni Center is the home of the remarkable Association of Former Students which nourishes the spirit and the financial resources of the University. Photograph by Mike Kellett. Courtesy Texas A&M University Photographic Services.

Aggie "elephants" slosh through the eternal fountain of youth. Photograph by Mike Kellett. Courtesy Texas A&M University Photographic Services.

"Howdy." Photograph by Jean Wulfson. Courtesy Texas A&M University Photographic Services.

The faces have changed over the years ...
but Aggies are still Aggies ...

Parsons Mounted Cavalry recalls a rich *Aggie* tradition. Courtesy Texas *A&M* University Photographic Services.

The Sam Houston Sanders Corps of Cadets Visitor Center helps preserve the history and traditions of Texas Aggies. Photograph by James Lyle. Courtesy Texas *A&M* University Photographic Services.

The John B. Connally Building, located off the campus, has replaced the "Systems Administration Building" as headquarters for Texas A&M's expanding network of Texas universities. Photograph by James Lyle. Courtesy Texas A&M University Photographic Services.

*One element hasn't changed,
though the vital ingredient that has made A&M
what it is, and what it will be . . .*

Courtesy Texas A&M University Archives.

Higher education, among other things, is an adventure in life. Photograph by Jean Wulfson. Courtesy Texas A&M University Photographic Services.

View of the University Library from the east. Photograph by Jim Bones.

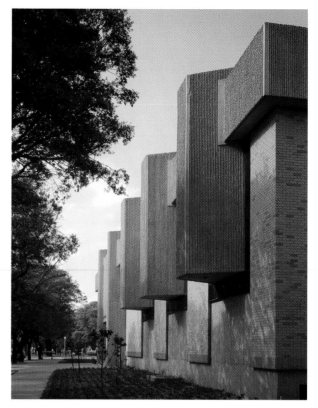

The A. P. Beutel Health Center, dedicated in *1974*. Photograph by Jim Bones.

Underground Food Court and Market. Courtesy Texas A&M University Photographic Services.

Student enrollment doubled between *1976* and *1996* to *43,000* students. Construction and expansion was a constant during those two decades. Photograph by Mike Kellett. Courtesy Texas A&M University Photographic Services.

The spirit of Texas A&M ...

Courtesy Texas A&M University Photographic Services.

Dr. Jarvis E. Miller, director of Texas Agricultural Experiment Station, became president of A&M on August 1, 1977. Courtesy Texas A&M University Archives.

president of A&M. Miller received his M.A. and Ph.D. degrees from Purdue University in agricultural economics. After a two-year stint in the air force, he returned to Texas A&M as assistant professor in livestock marketing. He became assistant director of the Agricultural Experiment Station in 1967, associate director in 1971, and director in 1972. Grounded in the tradition of service to society, President Miller sought to extend the role of the University to better serve the people of Texas and to improve the quality of the educational experience and programs.

With Miller's selection, a host of new administrative appointments occurred at both the system level and within the University. Chancellor Williams named William Clyde Freeman his vice chancellor for business. John C. Calhoun, formerly vice president for academic affairs, became the new vice chancellor for programs. James Bond was named vice chancellor for legal affairs, and Robert L. Walker, the vice president

for development, became vice chancellor for development. Lane B. Stephenson, who headed the University's news service, became assistant to the chancellor for public information.

President Miller then created his own University administration to replace that basically elevated to the system level by Chancellor Williams. Moody College in Galveston and state agencies, including the Extension Service and Experiment Stations, continued to report to President Miller. Dr. Neville Clark replaced Miller as director of the Texas Agricultural Experiment Station. Miller appointed Dr. John Mack Prescott, the dean of the College of Science, as his new vice president for academic affairs. Howard Vestal, formerly assistant vice president for business affairs, replaced his former boss, Thomas D. Cherry, as vice president for business affairs. Cherry, who directed the business office with tremendous energy and efficiency since the days of Earl Rudder, retired August 31, 1976. President Miller retained Professor Haskell Monroe as dean of faculties, then turned his hand vigorously to the tasks of the presidency.

Those tasks, however, became increasingly difficult.

It would be some time before the delicate balance between University and System offices could be established. A historic imbalance tended to prevail. Concerns of the University generally dominated those of the System. A strong chancellor and more contentious affiliated campuses including Prairie View A&M, Tarleton State College, and the Moody College in Galveston—supported by a growing constituency in the state legislature—began to challenge Texas A&M's hegemony in the system.

A Battalion editorial, seeking to reassure Aggies that the celestial order of things had not changed, inadvertently put its finger on the problem: Although the Texas A&M System "contains great diversity and land throughout Texas" its heart, mind, and muscle resides right here in College Station. Not only the academic institutions affiliated with Texas A&M but agencies such as the Texas Engineering Experiment Station, Texas Agricultural Experiment Station, Texas Agricultural Extension Service, and Texas Forest Service seemed to compete more and more with the "main" campus for funding and resources that had become more and more scarce and critical during times of growth. And there was, as there had been in the past, competition and conflict between the System and the main campus. Things were not in balance.

Chancellor Jack K. Williams resigned on January

23, 1979. President Miller and most A&M administrators expressed surprise. The regents appointed their chairman, Clyde H. Wells, acting chancellor. That spring gasoline prices, which the previous summer had dropped to nineteen cents a gallon, hit the federally mandated maximum of 68.9 cents a gallon in May and kept climbing. By June, gasoline had exceeded one dollar per gallon. The gas lines were long and tempers short. Gasoline rationing began. Inflation stood at 13 percent during the first quarter of 1979, and an American icon, John Wayne, died in May. But the Permanent University Fund's value now exceeded $1 billion.

On September 27, 1979, the regents appointed Frank W. R. Hubert, dean of the College of Education since 1969, as the new chancellor. When called to the board room, Dean Hubert thought he was to be consulted regarding procedures for the search for a new chancellor, instead, he got the job. In the spring, the regents reassigned the Extension Service and Experiment Station from the president's office to the authority of the chancellor.

Dr. Jarvis Miller, buffeted by funding pressures, problems related to faculty recruitment and growth, and controversies particularly involving women in the Corps (and Cadet Melanie Zentgraf in particular), tendered a tentative resignation to the board of regents in June, 1980. On July 9, he was relieved of duties as president. The next day the regents appointed Charles H. Samson, Jr., head of the department of civil engineering since 1964, acting president of Texas A&M University. Samson expressed surprise at his appointment but cited strong differences between the chancellor's office and the president's office for the organizational changes. He promised to pursue a "consult and decide" policy as interim president.

Later, the *Battalion* published an interview with Jarvis Miller and Frank Hubert. Chancellor Hubert suggested that the primary reason for the recent organizational changes was to allow the president of Texas A&M University the opportunity to focus on faculty, students, and programs and to leave administration of the state agencies and affiliated institutions to the chancellor. Dr. Miller regarded the change as evidence of the historic conflict between the University and the System, diced with a strong board of regents who in fact thought the regents rather than the chancellor or president should "run" the university and the system. Things were still not in balance, but a new order was imminent.

The pressures at the top overlay a campus caught in the throes of change, where traditions and the old order were confronting new and different growth. Frank Hubert commented later that by the close of the decade of the sixties, change at Texas A&M had become irrevocable. He attributed the foundations for change to three historic events: 1) the establishment of voluntary membership in the Corps of Cadets, 2) the unrestricted admission of women, and 3) the change in the name from Texas Agricultural and Mechanical College to Texas A&M University. Those changes all happened within a half-dozen years, but their consequences continued to unfold. Effective August 23, 1963, the Texas Legislature approved the change in name of the A&M College to Texas A&M University. Compulsory enrollment in the Corps of Cadets was abolished in September, 1965. The University catalog first acknowledged the open admission of women in 1971. Krueger Hall, the first women's dorm on campus, opened in 1972. That year women comprised 17 percent of the student body, the next year 22 percent, and the next 25 percent. That year, 1974, the Corps of Cadets admitted women and in the spring established W-1, the first woman's Corps unit. But "integration" of the Corps was still much more symbolic than real. Elite corps organizations such as the Aggie Band, the Ross Volunteers, Parsons Mounted Cavalry, and the Brigade Color Guard remained male bastions. Elephant Walk, when juniors assumed the prerogatives of seniors, remained a male tradition and privilege—until all of the above were challenged personally and in court in 1978 and 1979 by the previously mentioned female cadet, Melanie Zentgraf ('80). With that challenge some of the old walls of tradition began to crumble. That the conditions for change had been established earlier did not make change any easier. The eighties, though a difficult decade, were terribly interesting and exciting. The old Aggie bottle was being filled with a new wine.

Opposition to "Maggies" (female non-Corps Aggies), to "Waggies" (females in the Corps), and to "Frat-Rats" (fraternity and sorority members) declined precipitously after 1980. Pages of the *Battalion* soon dropped even the use of those rather denigrating terms. As the percentage of Corps membership relative to civilian enrollments declined and as the military services themselves included larger percentages of women, the controversies over women at Texas A&M, or women in the Corps of Cadets, or women in the Aggie Band became non-issues. Curiously,

President Frank E. Vandiver's vision for Texas A&M University: a true world university. Courtesy Texas A&M University Photographic Services.

"race" never seems to have become an issue, either in the seventies or the eighties. In 1984, Aggies elected Fred McClure, an African-American student, their student body president. A decade later, that former student body president became a regent of the Texas A&M University System.

Despite the recent campus controversies, frequent administrative reorganizations, and the problems of managing growth, the eighties came with a keen sense of anticipation and purpose. Being a part of Texas A&M University in any capacity was exciting. Problems could be solved, and controversies could be resolved. The Corps of Cadets established a second women's unit, Squadron 14. Contractors neared completion on the $24 million expansion of Kyle Field with seating for seventy thousand spectators. More than thirty thousand students were already enrolled at A&M. Accommodations and parking were even more scarce. A shuttle bus service began under University sponsorship. Enclosed multi-story parking garages helped solve the parking problems. Admissions had "overbooked" some six hundred students into campus housing for the fall of 1980. The University began building more dormitories for men and women, and the community responded with new apartment complexes. Stability and "balance" were being restored to the University and the System.

Chancellor Frank Hubert announced his retirement in March, 1981. The regents began a search both for a president of the University to replace acting president Samson and a chancellor to replace Frank Hubert. The presidential search attracted many candidates but none that seemed to quite meet the needs of the moment. Frank E. Vandiver recalled that at 7:00 A.M. one early August morning, he and his wife were having coffee at the president's home at North Texas State University when the phone rang. Frank Hubert was on the line. Vandiver asked Hubert if he was calling at such a terrible hour to tell him who had become the new president of Texas A&M. Hubert replied, "I hope I am talking to him."

But Vandiver had not been a candidate for the position. Hubert insisted that he consider it and call him back in thirty minutes. Vandiver called Norman Hackerman, the president of Rice University, under whom he had served as provost and academic vice president for many years. Hackerman told him he should consider the position. Vandiver returned Hubert's call and agreed to meet with regents H. R. 'Bum' Bright, and John M. Blocker in Dallas. At that meeting they told him he should go to Indianapolis to meet with Dr. Art Hansen at Purdue University, who, he was told, "is going to be the chancellor, next year." Vandiver insisted too that he visit with Texas A&M University and visit with the faculty. "This surprised the regents," he said. However, it coincided with Vandiver's basic premise that the faculty were after all the heart and soul of a university.

Dr. Frank E. Vandiver, a Rice University professor of history from 1955 to 1979, with experience as provost, academic vice president and acting president of Rice, and president of North Texas State University, began his duties as president of Texas A&M University in September, 1981. For a time, Vandiver said, he had thought of A&M as a "cow college" but having a daughter enrolled there and serious study greatly altered that all-too-common perception. Texas A&M had a good faculty with a national reputation in agriculture and engineering. It had a "coming" reputation in the sciences and a "fascinating" College of Education. It was a school where things could happen. And he determined to make it so.

Managing Change: A New Vision

A university president, Vandiver thought, "ought to have a vision," and it should be one that could clearly be articulated. During his first six months in office, he met faculty and administrators, studied programs and resources, and discovered that some of the "hidden" strengths of the school were its strong international connections and programs. It offered, he decided, the opportunity to become a true "world university" and should build to accommodate what he perceived as a new true international economic and social order.

Vandiver also wanted to enhance the quality and stature of the faculty, create new international associations, build a faculty and student body that reflected the ethnic and cultural diversity of Texas, and build structures for faculty governance and participation in developing programs. It would involve change. And change, he discovered, especially after an encounter with an angry former student who called him a "goddam liberal who was trying to change the University," was not always easy or popular. Vandiver's response was essentially that "Sir, if things were the same as when you were here, then we will not have been doing our job." To be sure, the issue was no longer change, but how to manage that change. Management required a "vision" shared as much as possible by the faculty, administrators, former students, and the students. The vision being formulated by President Vandiver and Texas A&M University would be shared and reinforced by the new chancellor. Regents succeeded in closing a "long courtship" with a former Purdue University president and engineer, Arthur Hansen. Hansen assumed the duties of chancellor in March, 1982. The eighties brought significant changes in the extent and character of Texas A&M University and in the nature of the Texas A&M University System.

A&M's System and, indeed, higher education in Texas began to experience internal strains and tensions from independent state colleges, branches of the University of Texas, and affiliated agencies and institutions of Texas A&M University. Each wanted to obtain a greater share of legislative appropriations for higher education and an apportionment of the Available University Fund (AUF) derived from the interest on accumulated oil revenues deposited into the Permanent University Fund since the discovery of Santa Rita in 1926.

That available fund, two-thirds of which went to the University of Texas and one-third to Texas A&M University under the 1931 agreement, had largely been allocated by those universities for the exclusive use of the main campuses. Both of Texas' flagship institutions experienced extremely rapid growth in the seventies and eighties. Both, in the nineties would have enrollments exceeding forty thousand students. Both found themselves depending more and more heavily on the AUF for construction and eventually for operating supplements as state appropriations failed to sustain either the growth or the quality enrichment programs sponsored by those universities. But while the two major Texas universities had their problems with growth, Texas' smaller colleges and universities were even more hard-pressed because of their sole dependence on biennial legislative appropriations.

And those colleges, predominately Prairie View A&M University, chafed under their relative deprivation and lusted after an equitable allocation from the PUF. African-American state legislators, especially Wilhelmina Delco from Austin, had been trying for years to get additional PUF funding for Prairie View. Finally, in September, 1982, a threatened legal suit against Texas A&M University and the University of Texas forced a resolution to the problem.

Hansen, with the concurrence and support of the University of Texas, met with Representative Delco and worked out an agreement apportioning a specified amount of the Available Fund to Prairie View. Introduced by Delco and approved by the legislature, HMR 19 went to the voters for approval in 1984 as a constitutional amendment. It provided Prairie View an "equitable portion" of Texas A&M's portion of the Available Fund, included a $60 million supplemental fund provided by the University of Texas to be paid out over ten years, and more importantly, established a permanent state construction fund for all colleges and universities.

Wilhelmina Delco said that working with Dr. Hansen was like a "breath of fresh air." Hansen said that a lawsuit could have frozen the use of the Available Fund and "would have brought both UT and A&M to their knees. . . . I did not come to Texas to preside over a second-class institution or a branch of a second-class institution."

The competition for resources affected not only Texas A&M University but the University of Texas System and higher education in Texas in general. Paradoxically, the new competition for shared funding contributed to an end of the ancient "Battle of the Universities" and a new accord between Texas A&M

University and the University of Texas. Thus, many of the bones of contention that had confounded Texas A&M during its first century were being laid to rest early in the second. There were, of course, new problems, new issues, and new controversies for the new century, but Texas A&M was now planning its future and not wrestling with its past.

The past, of course, could never be wholly dismissed. As a part of the past, the Texas A&M University Board of Regents and former students tended to regard the athletic programs as their own turf. Frank Vandiver recalls vividly when the board of regents informed him that they had replaced head football coach Tom Wilson with Jackie Sherrill. Vandiver had not been involved. He protested at what he described as a stormy meeting with the board of regents. The president, not the regents, he told them, must run the University and that included the athletic program. While he acknowledged the board's final authority, he said if he were excluded in the future, he would tender his resignation—and wrote a letter to that effect.

Vandiver then called a special convocation of the entire faculty of the University—a first in the history of the school—to get faculty input into a resolution of the problem. He challenged the faculty that if they were not supportive he would tender his resignation at their request. Although the faculty were largely speechless at this unprecedented turn of events, no motion either of support or condemnation occurred and the meeting adjourned. But it led, Vandiver said, to the realization that the administration needed to organize a structure for systematic faculty input into issues and problems confronting the University. A number of faculty led by Thomas J. Kozik, a professor of mechanical engineering, urged Vandiver to consider a faculty senate. Vandiver appointed a committee headed by Claude Davis. The result was the creation of the Faculty Senate—perhaps one of the most important changes instituted by President Vandiver.

The Senate assumed responsibility for course approvals, the development of a core curriculum, program planning, and became a two-way conduit for information and input between faculty and administration. It could become a thorn in the president's side, Vandiver admitted, but it was absolutely necessary both for recruitment and good governance.

The position of dean of faculties, created by Dr. Jack Williams, became integral to the Faculty Senate. The first dean of faculties, Haskell Monroe, left Texas A&M to become president of the University of Texas–

El Paso. Dr. Clinton A. Phillips, a professor of finance who had come to A&M from Tulane University in 1967 and had served as head of the department of finance and a short term of acting dean of the College of Business Administration, replaced Monroe as dean of faculties, and later he also assumed the duties of associate provost.

Vandiver named Gordon Eaton, former associate chief of the U.S. Geologic Service, dean of the College of Geosciences in August, 1981, replacing Earl Cook, who retired. Replacing Charles E. McCandless, Eaton then became provost and vice president for academic affairs in 1983. Eaton supervised the deans and department heads and worked closely with faculty. He wanted particularly to "computerize" the University to keep abreast of rapid changes in modern technology, to raise student admission standards, and to control "rampant" growth. He sought, in effect, to "control" change but advised that "when nothing is changing" the institution is "dead on its feet." Texas A&M would never be "dead on its feet."

Eaton worked very closely with Clint Phillips, who described his role as an "ombudsman" between the faculty and the administration to help channel faculty into the decision-making processes. Phillips helped organize the tenure and promotion processes, ameliorated salary complaints, organized faculty and administrator recruitment, and provided arbitration and resolution for disputes involving sexual harassment and minority recruitment. By 1990, when he ended his service as dean of faculties, Texas A&M University had become a far different place than that at which he had arrived in 1967. Even Earl Rudder, Phillips said, would never have believed that A&M would have grown so great.

One of Phillips's responsibilities was to "increase the diversity of the faculty" under a program instituted by President Vandiver with a special $4 million commitment from the board of regents for minority faculty recruitment. That program began, Vandiver recalled, when Professor Ruth Schaffer in the department of sociology challenged him to do something about minority student and faculty recruitment. Vandiver responded by appointing Schaffer to head a committee to make recommendations. The end product was a concerted and generally successful effort to recruit women, Hispanic, and African-American faculty and students such that the A&M profile would better reflect the realities of Texas society and create an enriched learning environment.

Changes in the System

Enrichment also occurred on other levels. Vandiver, with Chancellor Hansen's approval, sought to resolve the problems caused by the transfer of authority over Agricultural and Engineering Experiment Stations and Extension Services from the University to the System. Many faculty were fully or partly employed, for example, by the Engineering Experiment Station. Their "boss" could be wholly the chancellor or sometimes both the chancellor and the president if the individual was on part-time research and part-time teaching. Research projects were in effect funded at the System level and virtually divorced from teaching. But teaching and research were, in the minds of most educators, inseparable. It was, Vandiver thought, a confusing and debilitating situation. Although he could not convince the chancellor to return the research and extension agencies to the University, Hansen and Vandiver did resolve the problem by creating two new faculty-administrative positions.

Donald McDonald, a professor of petroleum engineering, became acting dean of engineering and deputy chancellor for engineering upon the retirement of Dean Fred J. Benson. Dr. Perry Adkisson, deputy chancellor for agriculture, Texas A&M's first member of the National Academy of Science, and a recipient of the Humbolt Award for outstanding contributions to American agriculture also became acting dean of the College of Agriculture upon the retirement of Dean H. O. Kunkel. Thus, the bridging of gap between the University and the System, which had given past presidents and chancellors such misery, began.

That bridge became more permanent with the selection of four deputy chancellors. Dr. Charles J. Arntzen, another member of the National Academy of Sciences and a distinguished professor of biochemistry and biophysics, was named dean of the College of Agriculture and deputy chancellor for agriculture and life sciences. Herbert H. Richardson became deputy chancellor for engineering and dean of the college. Eddie J. Davis became deputy chancellor for finance and administration, and James B. Bond became deputy chancellor of external affairs and legal counsel.

When Arthur Hansen resigned as chancellor in January, 1986, the regents appointed Perry Lee Adkisson to the position. With a doctorate in entomology from Kansas State University and graduate and undergraduate degrees from the University of Arkansas, Adkisson, who had joined the A&M faculty in 1958, joined his

When Herbert H. Richardson served as chancellor of Texas A&M, he saw the job required organization, planning, and integrating resources. Photograph by James Lyle. Courtesy Texas A&M University Photographic Services.

scholarly instincts and A&M experience with a quietly and determinedly efficient management expertise. Adkisson linked the role of higher education directly to the economic welfare of the society. "There is a strong, direct link between scientific research and development on the one hand and a solid economy and high employment on the other," he believed. Thus he treated the role of the Texas A&M University System as a state-wide and even national responsibility.

Before he resigned on January 1, 1991, to return to teaching and research, he was largely responsible for establishing an Institute of Biosciences and Technology in Houston, the movement of the system offices off-campus into the Bryan-College Station community, the opening of system offices in Austin and Houston, and substantial funding increases for system institutions. He also supervised the doubling of the "System" itself from four to eight educational institutions. When he stepped down, Edward A. Hiler, professor and former head of the department of agricultural engineering and deputy chancellor for academic program planning filled the position as interim chancellor. Meanwhile, the regents searched for a new chancellor and found him on campus—Herbert H. Richardson.

Richardson grew up in the engineering environment of his father's machine shop in Bridgeton, Maine. His father wanted him to be an engineer. He decided to go into physics at Colby College but after one year switched to engineering and to Massachusetts Institute of Technology in Cambridge, Massachusetts where he earned his undergraduate and post-graduate degrees in engineering.

A distinguished military graduate of the MIT Reserve Officers Training Corps, he served his active duty at the Army Ballistics Research Laboratory before returning to MIT as assistant professor of mechanical engineering. After a tour in Washington, D.C. as chief scientist of the Department of Transportation, he returned to MIT to become head of the Department of Mechanical Engineering, and later associate dean of the college. He joined the Texas A&M faculty in 1984 as deputy chancellor of engineering and dean of the College of Engineering.

Richardson considered A&M an "intriguing" and promising situation. Engineering programs had tremendous resources under the direction variously of the College of Engineering, the Engineering Experiment Station, and the Engineering Extension Service. But the engineering components were independent and isolated from each other and often competed for resources. There were strong walls between departments within the college, but a powerful "can-do" attitude.

Richardson remembers his first meeting with engineering department heads. "It was a real quiet meeting," he said. Finally, one of the heads spoke up and said, "Tell us what you want us to do, and we'll do it!" That has been the Aggie way.

His job in engineering was to integrate the state engineering agencies with the college, eliminate duplicative centers, remove barriers between departments, promote interdisciplinary studies, and provide research incentives and "sharing" for departments and individual faculty members. During his tenure as dean and vice chancellor between 1985 and 1991, engineering program expenditures rose from $57 to $122 million annually, and the College of Engineering endowment rose from $10 to $40 million.

When Richardson became chancellor of the Texas A&M University System on August 29, 1991, he saw his job similar in spirit to that required in the College of Engineering—organization, planning, and integrating resources, while preserving the integrity and in-

dependence of the members of the system. There really wasn't much "System" to the Texas A&M University System when he arrived in 1985.

The Texas A&M University System had long been confined to four major institutions with A&M being the central campus in terms of enrollment and funding. Prairie View A&M University, Tarleton State University, and until 1965 Arlington State College (now the University of Texas at Arlington) functioned as autonomous and rather distant institutions under the A&M "umbrella." Texas A&M University at Galveston, first organized as the Moody College of Marine Sciences and Maritime Resources, continued to serve largely as a satellite campus of the main University. That "System" changed markedly in 1989 when four major Texas public institutions of higher education were assigned to the Texas A&M University System by the Texas Legislature.

Laredo State University, Corpus Christi State University, Texas A&I University at Kingsville, and West Texas State University in Canyon became associated with Texas A&M. The eight universities and campuses comprising the A&M System now employed about 20,000 persons, enrolled over 175,000 students (regular and extension) and had a combined annual budget in excess of $1 billion.

> The Texas A&M University System is a federation of state universities and agencies; focused on technology, science and management; enriched by the arts and humanities; serving people through education, leadership development, research and service.

Member institutions of the Texas A&M University System are not branches of A&M. Each institution has its own character, constituency, and integrity, but each can draw upon the others' strengths. Chancellor Richardson worked to transfer some of the strengths of Texas A&M University to member institutions, such as the Aggie ability to develop leadership, the Aggie sense of loyalty and cohesiveness, and A&M's stress on quality. Effective September 1, 1993, the regents more fully integrated the new components of the System into the "Aggie System" by changing the name of Laredo State University to Texas A&M International University, Corpus Christi State University to Texas A&M University–Corpus Christi, and Texas A&I University to Texas A&M University–Kingsville. Some, particularly at Texas A&I, protested the name changes, but the overriding mission had not changed.

The mission of Texas A&M University and the System is education. True to the old Agricultural and

Mechanical College heritage, the System stresses education and training as a collaborative enterprise between the member institutions and industry, particularly in the realm of agriculture and engineering.

While students and faculty entered into new participatory roles in the life of Texas A&M University, the role and participation of former students, once a largely off-campus and athletic-events oriented independent body, also became more closely integrated with the academic development of the University.

The Former Students Association

The Former Students Association, first organized as an "Association of Ex-Cadets" in June, 1880, grew into a vigorous, sometimes boisterous, occasionally troublesome, and largely unfocused alumni organization by the close of World War II. By 1976, Texas A&M's former student association became not just a twelfth man cheering the team on to victories but a fourth estate of Texas A&M University which infused the spirit and much of the money to support the students, faculty, and administration.

The conversion of the former students association began in part with E. E. McQuillen's efforts to maintain communications with A&M students fighting in battlefields around the world and association support for Muster ceremonies, wherever in the world two or more Aggies might be together on April 21. After the war, financial aid for the veterans and new students crowding into the campus became an important need. Former students and many faculty were making independent loans to students. McQuillen and Dick Hervey, who succeeded McQuillen as director of the former students association in 1947, made arrangements for the A&M College financial aid office to manage a student loan program funded by former student gifts.

Over time it became very clear that former student financial support was simply inadequate to meet the needs, but the former students wanted to help. In 1959, the former students conducted a fund-raising experiment—making a gift to Texas A&M independent of membership fees in the association. The fund drive increased participation by former students in "giving," but gifts averaged only $12.81 per contributor, recalls Richard O. "Buck" Weirus, who was then heading the Aggie fund drive in San Antonio and was a member of the board of directors of the former students association.

The next year President Rudder and Dick Hervey asked Buck Weirus to meet with them in Bandera, where they invited him to come to Texas A&M as assistant executive director of the association in charge of fund raising. Weirus, who was born Richard Weirus Lund, arrived in San Antonio in 1934 with his mother, who opened a hose mending and reweaving business, where he worked and learned a trade. Friends of Weirus said "the uniforms and ROTC" led him to enroll at Texas A&M in 1938. In 1943, he graduated and went directly to active duty, arriving at LaHavre, France in the fall of 1944 for duty with the 20th Army Corps and service along the Rhine and Mosel rivers. In 1945, now with the 3rd Army, he was transferred back to the States for transhipment to the Pacific theater. The war ended in August, and Weirus left active duty in October, 1946, to return to San Antonio and the weaving business.

As did many other veterans, he returned to active duty during the Korean conflict, and in 1955, he left the military for service with the San Antonio utilities system. He got fund-raising experience as San Antonio's United Fund chairman and in a fund drive for the Methodist Church. In 1959, he headed the Aggie fund drive and also left the city works for a private advertising firm. In 1961, he came to A&M. It was like coming home.

Weirus replaced Dick Hervey as director of the former student association in 1964. After canvassing the needs and possibilities, Weirus and his directors decided that the former students association needed to separate fund raising from alumni dues and lifetime memberships, as were customary in most alumni organizations. From 1965 to 1968, the association launched a fund drive tied to the expansion of the football stadium at Kyle Field. The drive emphasized "annual giving" and focused on $100 gifts. Weirus borrowed from a "YMCA Man" plaque to invent the Century Club plaque awarded for $100 gifts. Former student Royce E. Wisenbaker ('39) donated $10,000 for the purchase of the plaques which were first awarded in 1966. Later, silver ($250), gold ($500), and diamond ($1,000) level awards were made for Century Club gifts.

While a football stadium drive provided the initial impetus for a sustained program of annual giving, student aid and welfare had long been a former student concern. The association decided to fund scholarships for needy students. In 1965, association board members Royce Wisenbaker and Buck Weirus went to President Rudder with a $25,000 scholarship endowment check. Rudder was hesitant to accept the gift, believing that it might come with strings attached and that he might be inheriting yet another board of directors.

With those reservations overcome, the former students hired Robert L. Walker from Pepperdine University to become executive director of the former students association with responsibility for the Presidential Endowed Scholarship program. These fund raising initiatives soon led to the organization of the Texas A&M Development Foundation and substantial gifts for faculty teaching awards and building endowments. Annual former student giving rose from about $178,000 in 1960, to more than $1 million in 1970, with average annual gifts of $4 million since 1980.

The Texas Aggie, which Buck Weirus described as a nondescript "terrible" tabloid when he arrived for duty with the former students association in 1961, became a polished, highly effective magazine. Beginning with the work of editor Karl Elmquist, a professor in the Department of English, *The Texas Aggie* evolved into an attractive and informative alumni journal. Joe Buser ('59) became the first full-time staff editor, followed by Connie Eckard ('55), and after 1971, Jerry C. Cooper ('63).

Jerry Cooper describes *The Texas Aggie* as "more than words and pictures on paper,"

> *The Texas Aggie*, official publication of the Association of Former Students, is more than words and pictures on paper. In many ways, it is the catalog of the people, events, and circumstances that make up the essence of the "Aggie Spirit."
>
> While the Corps of Cadets is the "Keeper of the Aggie Spirit," *The Texas Aggie* magazine has for 72 years helped preserve A&M history and keep alumni ties strong by informing Aggies of the progress of their alma mater and updating them on accomplishments of their Aggie friends.
>
> Speeches are transitory and meaningful words are often lost in the passage of time. *The Texas Aggie* captures these words and records them for posterity. The magazine is a primary reference for those searching A&M history and seeking to collect the stories of Texas A&M University for a book, video, or other publication.
>
> Although the Aggie Spirit has truly "never been told," bits and pieces of the "Spirit" can be found in *The Texas Aggie* magazines published since 1921.

> Jerry C. Cooper
> July 4, 1993

Weirus became Executive Director Emeritus of the former students association in 1980 and in 1993, received the Distinguished Alumnus Award from the former students. James R. (Randy) Matson ('67), a marketing major, outstanding athlete, and gold medal Olympic champion took the reigns as executive director of the association. In the next score of years, membership in the former students association, reflecting the phenomenal growth of the University, doubled from about a hundred thousand to two hundred thousand members—each individual linked by that indescribable bond called the Aggie spirit to the continuing welfare of the University.

In the fall of 1987, *The Texas Aggie*, Randy Matson, and staff of the former students association moved into munificent new quarters at the Clayton W. Williams, Jr. ('54) Alumni Center. That year former students and friends gave a total of $39,148,239 to Texas A&M. The next year William H. Mobley became the twentieth president of Texas A&M University, replacing Frank Vandiver who stepped down to resume work on his first love—military history.

Preparing for the Twenty-first Century

Bill Mobley, who served as executive deputy chancellor from 1986–88, came to Texas A&M in 1980 to head the department of management. In 1983, he became dean of the College of Business Administration, replacing Dean William E. Muse, who accepted the position as president of the University of Akron (Ohio). Building upon the initiatives of his predecessors, John R. Pearson and Muse, Mobley "ministered" Texas A&M's College of Business Administration (in existence for less than two decades) into one of the most dynamic and expanding business colleges in the United States and one with a strong focus on the international business community.

Born in Akron, Ohio, Mobley received his undergraduate degree in psychology and economics from Denison University. From 1964 to 1967, he had a tour of duty with Pittsburgh Plate Glass (PPG) working the "college recruiting circuit" before enrolling in the University of Maryland where he received the masters and doctorate degrees in industrial-organizational psychology. He went back to PPG for a time, had a "teaching experience" at Carnegie Mellon, and got excited about it. He then joined the faculty of the University of South Carolina where he directed the Center for Management and Organizational Research. He left South Carolina to come to Texas.

William H. Mobley, formerly dean of the College of Business Administration and the twentieth president of A&M, chats with students near the Academic Building. "Education like business," President Mobley said, "is becoming a global process." Courtesy Texas A&M University Photographic Services.

Mobley had a vision for Texas A&M University, as did his predecessor, Frank Vandiver. It brought the "world university" concept of Vandiver into sharper focus. Mobley saw that education, like business, was becoming and would be in the future a global process. The information network relies upon international resources. Texas, he said, is a "global state" with strong international connections and opportunities. International educational processes, like global business, require responding to diverse cultures and conditions. Texas A&M's graduates must be prepared to work and to compete in a global setting of a rapidly changing world. Diversity and flexibility in education and in business have become political and economic necessities. It is this new world of the twenty-first century for which Texas A&M must prepare its graduates.

Mobley thought that Texas and Texas A&M University were admirably equipped to meet the chal-

lenges of that new world. He observed that A&M produced a good graduate—respected and recognized by external markets. The military tradition instilled a sense of personal discipline. A&M students, by virtue of their military experiences—from the time of the Spanish-American War into the more current actions in Granada, and Desert Shield/Desert Storm in the Middle East (in which three Aggies lost their lives)—were generally well-versed in training and in experience in international affairs. Aggies in agricultural production and petroleum production in particular had a history of global involvement. Moreover, Texas was itself a state with large and diverse resources and international connections. But there were limitations, the proverbial wolves lurking in the bushes.

Texas A&M could not be all things to all people. It must conserve and focus its resources. It had an inherent indisposition to change. Faculty and administrators tended to operate from old and possibly outdated

E. Dean Gage, DVM, a pioneer in spinal and neural surgery, served as associate dean of the College of Veterinary Medicine before service as provost and interim president of Texas A&M University. Courtesy Texas A&M University Photographic Services.

paradigms, models, and hypotheses. What worked in the past would not necessarily work in the future. Internally, Texas A&M needed to cut through the traditional disciplinary walls and to forge new links and associations with other institutions—as, he added, Texas A&M was now doing with the University of Texas and with affiliated universities of the Texas A&M System.

Mobley, optimistic about the future, noted that the limited financial resources of the eighties, occasioned by the collapse in oil prices, a state and national recession, and a university growth rate that invariably exceeded state funding, would soon be in better supply. The state and national economy were rebounding in the nineties. A capital fund raising campaign styled "Capturing the Spirit" neared its $500 million goal long before the 1996 target date. These funds, coming largely from alumni and friends of A&M, would provide essential resources in needed areas of university life. Moreover, resources in the Available University Fund were improving. Some of the financial storm clouds of the eighties were beginning to give way to sunnier days in the nineties.

Mobley believed that sound fiscal management, coupled with enrollment management and qualitative recruitment programs, would both alleviate financial problems and enhance the quality of programs. Texas A&M must "think strategically," identify and assess areas of opportunity, be increasingly sensitive to the changing needs of students and its external constituents, capitalize on its strong history of research and grant procurement, broaden its international focus, and become, like society around it, a more diverse and perceptive community. The rate of change in the world is accelerating, he said, and students entering into that world must be better prepared both to seize the opportunities brought by change and to better manage change. Future workers, he surmised, may very well have multiple careers—a single academic program or university degree will be less and less likely to qualify a student for life's work. Thus, the challenges of and changes in higher education and at Texas A&M University would become greater.

The growing University in College Station contained a tremendous amount of human energy. What it did not seem to have enough of for the twenty-first century was the electrical energy to power the buildings and facilities that had almost doubled in the past quarter-century. Texas A&M University regents authorized University officials to request proposals from prospective contractors for the construction of a $120 million cogeneration electrical plant, the largest construction project in the school's history. In May, 1993, Chancellor Richardson queried President Mobley about the need for the additional plant. In August, Richardson resigned as chancellor to return to the classroom. On August 28, 1993, the regents named Mobley chancellor of the Texas A&M University System. Regent Chairman Ross D. Margraves, Jr., explained the selection of Mobley: "He's been a great president, and he'll make an even better chancellor." At the same time regents approved the appointment of E. Dean Gage to interim president of Texas A&M University.

Gage, a native of San Saba who received both a B.S. degree and a D.V.M. (Doctor of Veterinary Medicine) at Texas A&M in 1966, had been serving as Mobley's senior vice president and provost. Gage, a pioneer in spinal and neural surgery at Auburn University, was a member of the Texas A&M veterinary faculty between 1969 and 1979 before becoming chairman of the Veterinary Teaching Hospital at the University of Tennessee and head of its department of urban practice. In 1982, he returned to Texas A&M as associate dean of veterinary medicine before assuming the job as provost and vice president for academic affairs and then senior vice president and provost. President Gage appointed A. Benton Cocanougher, dean of the College of Business, to fill his old position on an interim basis.

Gage said that "the mission of the University must be to continue to prepare its students for the challenges of a changing world." He pointed to the study abroad programs, the A&M campuses and programs in Japan, Italy, and Mexico City, the large number of foreign students enrolled at Texas A&M, and the cooperative agreements with foreign universities as evidence of Texas A&M University's efforts to enlarge its own global environment. The enlarged context of university administration requires, he said, that the administrator be a good oral and written communicator. That person must be "astute to the politics of the external constituents" while being closely tuned to the interests and aspirations of the faculty, staff, and students. The job requires vision, organizational skills, and tremendous energy. Gage believed that the course had been set. In the foreseeable future there would be no dramatic "changes in direction." Texas A&M would continue to serve its undergraduate students while enhancing its graduate and professional programs within the context of a rapidly changing world.

Change presented both challenge and opportunities. One of the opportunities, approved by the board of regents in January, 1994, was to sign a contract for construction of a new Texas A&M University power plant. Another change was when the campus began to "privatize" food services. This altered a more than 100-year plus tradition of university stewardship begun by Bernard Sbisa in 1878. The campus, students, and faculty roiled with controversy over "multiculturalism," "gay rights," "faculty governance," "women in the Texas Aggie Marching Band," "parking," and simply finding an opening for a class and a place to live. Aggies went to the Persian Gulf War. The Soviet Union collapsed and the Cold War ended. NAFTA and the European Union began, and a new global awareness began to form. On campus the *Battalion* celebrated its 100th birthday.

Battalion Celebrates its 100th Anniversary

Editor Chris Whitley noted in a special edition that the first issue of the *Battalion* appeared on October 1,

1893. The first student editor, E. L. Bruce, promised to do everything in his power to make the newspaper, "lively, interesting, and instructive." And Whitley commented a hundred years later, "From victory to tragedy, through change and tradition, Texas A&M has grown with the *Battalion* since 1893."

Mark Evans, city editor for the *Battalion*, admitted that in preparing for the 100th anniversary, the staff had learned much about Texas A&M and about the *Battalion*:

> We learned that this University has seen many changes during the 100 years that the *Battalion* has existed. When the newspaper first rolled off of the presses in 1893, only 500 students attended Texas A&M College, and all were members of the Corps. A&M's current enrollment surpasses 43,000 students and 1,900 are Corps members.
>
> We learned that some of these changes have not come without controversy.
>
> We learned that A&M has many interesting anecdotes about what the school used to be like, and . . . we learned that controversy has become a tradition here at the *Battalion*.

Perhaps, in keeping with the admonition of the *Battalion*'s first editor, E. L. Bruce, Texas A&M University had been "a lively, interesting, and instructive" place since its establishment. Sometimes things seemed to get a bit too lively, but it made life a lot more interesting. One of the most interesting and instructive developments in recent times had to do with the establishment of a presidential library on the Texas A&M University campus.

The George Bush Presidential Library

After President George Bush lost his bid for reelection in November, 1992, and upon the completion of his term, he and Mrs. Bush returned home to Houston, Texas. In time, President Bush decided that Texas A&M University would become the site of the George Bush Presidential Library. It would be the benchmark for Texas A&M University's entry into the next century.

Scheduled to begin operations in 1997, the George Bush Presidential Library will become the tenth such presidential library in the United States. It is expected to become a major library and learning center in the twenty-first century, not only for Texas A&M University but for the nation and the world community.

President and Mrs. George Bush break ground for the George Bush Presidential Library. Photograph by James Lyle. Courtesy Texas A&M University Photographic Services.

Model of the George Bush Presidential Library Center. Courtesy George Bush Presidential Library.

The George Bush Presidential Library Center will chronicle the history of President Bush's time, including his presidency and his long public service career in the United Nations, China, the Central Intelligence Agency, Congress, as vice president, and as world leader.

It will be a living, enduring, and vital enterprise. As a part of the National Archives, the library holdings will be accessible to scholars and students from around the world. They will write the history of one of the most exciting periods in world politics—the demise of communism and what has been termed the creation of a "new world order." These facilities and programs will afford national and international scholars the opportunity to assemble for study, research, and conferences.

> In this presidential library, at Texas A&M University, you will find documentation for some of the most revolutionary changes that the world has ever seen take place. Whether it is the peace talks . . . or whether it is the unification in Germany . . . whether it is the decline and fall of the Soviet Empire . . . whether it is the historic precedence-setting coalition for Desert

Storm. All of that will be reflected with accurate detail in the library for scholars to make their own conclusion.

> —George Bush

The Presidential Library also includes a museum, archives, meeting rooms, classrooms, auditoria, administrative offices, and space for additional university programs. New university programs organized as an adjunct to the library include the George Bush School of Government and Public Service, Center for Presidential Studies, and Center for Public Leadership Studies.

Something Old and Something New

There was progress. There was change. Sometimes the changes seemed too rapid, unfocused, inexplicable. It seemed sometimes that the University became a bit too lively, and that controversy became a tradition at Texas A&M University. One of those times was the spring, 1994. The new University power generation contract came under close public scrutiny.

Former President George Bush. Courtesy George Bush Presidential Library.

The issue of privatizing food services became increasingly controversial. Faculty fell into contention over offering a required course in "multiculturism." The Texas Rangers began an investigation of aspects of the University's business and financial dealings. The University regents authorized an independent audit.

In April, the regents named Dr. Ray M. Bowen, president of Texas A&M University. Bowen ('58) received a master's degree at California Institute of Technology in 1959 and his doctorate in mechanical engineering at Texas A&M University in 1961. He had diverse academic and administrative experiences ranging from the University of Kentucky to Oklahoma State University, where he served as provost and interim president before accepting the Texas A&M position. Ross Margraves, chairman of the board of regents commented that:

> Dr. Bowen's experience in leading a major state
> university and his background in engineering and

science make him ideally suited to lead Texas A&M University into the new century and into a new era of accomplishments built on its past and present.

Bowen said that returning to one's own university as its president was a special opportunity and the fulfillment of a dream. He wanted to be known as the "academic president" of Texas A&M University. He promised to stress the development of a diverse academic, faculty, and student environment to better prepare A&M students for the new century ahead.

Ray Bowen understood Texas A&M University and the needs of modern higher education. Having academic experience at A&M and Cal Tech, he spent much of his teaching career at Rice University, moving from assistant professor to professor of mechanical engineering between 1967 and 1983. He served as dean of the College of Engineering at the University of Kentucky for six years before accepting the position of assistant director of engineering and deputy assistant director for engineering of the National Science Foundation. He moved from there to the position of provost and vice president for academic affairs at Oklahoma State University, before being named interim president at that institution. Bowen immediately began applying a steadying hand to the helm of Texas A&M University.

But there were tough decisions to be made and a lot of turbulence on the campus and off. Within weeks of his arrival on campus, Ross Margraves, the chairman of the board of regents, resigned and was replaced by a new chairwoman, Mary Nan West. In June, Bill Mobley resigned the chancellorship to return to the classroom. That same month President Bowen made a number of new appointments to key management and financial positions. In July, the regents named Barry Thompson as the new chancellor. The faculty became restive arguing that the faculty had not been consulted in administrative changes of such magnitude. All this in the first six months of 1994.

Bowen's new "boss" and A&M System head, Barry Thompson, had broad Texas A&M and System experiences. He served as president of Tarleton State University before accepting the same position at West Texas State University. While at Tarleton, Thompson reported to the A&M chancellor. While at West Texas State University, Thompson offered his blessings and guidance when the University joined the Texas A&M University System. Thompson earned a doctorate in education in 1972 from Texas A&M University, an associate degree from Tarleton State in 1956, a bachelor's degree

Texas A&M University President Ray Bowen. Photograph by James Lyle. Courtesy Texas A&M University Photographic Services.

Chancellor Barry Thompson, former president of Tarleton State University and West Texas State University, brought "System experience," and a strong touch of humanity to Texas A&M University. Photograph by James Lyle. Courtesy Texas A&M University Photographic Services.

from Texas Tech in 1958, and a master's degree from East Texas State University in 1961. The latter became a part of the Texas A&M University System during Thompson's first year as chancellor. Thompson seemed groomed for the job of Aggie chancellor.

With the chancellorship, as with the presidency, there were a lot of decisions to be made and a lot of turbulence to be managed. Thompson looked ahead rather than at the rocky shoals, the politics, the audits, and the problems through which Texas A&M and the System seemed to be sailing at the moment. "The urgent business of the Texas A&M University System," he said, "is continuing to provide the best possible education for our students."

> Education is about values. Education is about civility, about literature, the arts. It's about the highest expression mankind can make.

Thompson initiated "Operation Lone Star" to re-affirm the mission of Texas A&M's seven universities and its related state agencies.

Chancellor Thompson and President Bowen worked to repair the damaged public image that the

University seemed to have acquired in the media and to clearly and forcefully inform the people and the legislature about the mission and responsibilities of Texas A&M University and the System. Both stressed the mission of Texas A&M as being education to train leaders—not managers. Both began the unremitting struggle for improved state funding in a political climate that threatened budget cuts rather than the increases needed to fund the expanding size and mission of the University and its associated campuses.

In the latter effort, Aggies, as they had in the past, made their own private contributions to the future welfare of their University. The "Capturing the Spirit Campaign," which began some years earlier as an effort to provide academic enrichment beyond the means available under existing funding, neared the goal of $400 million by August, 1994. By 1996, Texas A&M completed a capital fund campaign that would top the targeted $500 million. The Aggie spirit meant much more than "Beating the hell out of t.u." It meant, as Senator William Moore had explained before the 1974 summer graduating class, "an unsurpassed love for this institution."

In the fall, things settled a bit. The faculty and administrators wrestled with multiculturism, minority recruiting, and budgeting. Students attended classes, took exams, and went to bonfire and yell practice and, when necessary, to Silver Taps.

A ceremony close to all Aggies, Silver Taps represents a final goodbye.

A quiet hush has fallen, broken only by the distant sounds of traffic, the constant chirp of crickets, and the soft rhythmic slap of the rope against the flagpole as it stands at half-staff. A silence born of ritual reverence overwhelms the audience. It is a silence in which one's thoughts seem loud. Memories come over those of us there to remember a friend, to once again say farewell. This is his place, and now is his time. All that he stood for is embodied in this ceremony. It is a gathering of friends and acquaintances, all there to pay tribute in their own special way. A symbol of this place and these people, an event unequaled by any other.

Softly comes the drum, announcing the beginning. Unseen in the dark the honor guard approaches. Their quiet cadenced steps bring all of us one step closer to the moment we have come to see yet wish would never occur. Once again, we all breathe deep, and once again we remember the man, the boy, our friend. Going over and over in our minds are the memories of fun and laughter, the looks and expressions, never to be seen again. Slowly they move closer to their destination. Overhead in the moonlight is the dome, never so beautiful in the bright light of day. Somehow the soft ethereal light transforms the building into a shrine, a symbol of those gone before, something that will be there after we are all gone. Permanence. Tradition.

The slow count begins. The guard moves into final position in the darkness. We are far back in the crowd and out of sight of the movement, but we all can see them in our minds. We sense as they raise their rifles skyward. Though we know it is coming, the first volley of shots shake us to the core. A torrent of emotion is released, pent up for weeks, hiding in the deep recesses of our souls. Once again we are helpless as children, inconsolable in the face of loss. Temporarily distracted by the sound of wind through the wings of frightened birds leaving their evening roost in the trees that surround us, returning to the moment with the second, and then third volley. The world stops. Thousands of people with little in common are bonded in that moment. It becomes a definition of who we are—who he was. We mourn again and again.

Gently but clearly the horns caress the first notes in the stillness. Their sad tomes at once both rent and heal the wounds of the heart and soul. While mourning, we remember. Different memories for different friends, all bittersweet in the joy and sadness. Loss countered by achievement, tragedy overwhelmed by the blessing of his friendship. Twice more the notes are repeated as we retreat into our memories, holding each other, affirming our bond. The last notes fade like smoke on the soft breeze. The ceremony is over. Let the healing begin. Let the memories never fade.

C. Matthew Gardner
September 5, 1995

The Aggie football team went undefeated (10-0-1) for the 1994 season—that had not happened since 1956. But even that was not as happy an event as it might have been. Texas A&M University had been slapped with a five-year NCAA probation, which included no televised games or bowl games for 1994.

The *Battalion* summarized 1994 as "a tough year." Reveille VI had been puppy-napped by UT students but finally returned alive and well. The five-year NCAA probation rankled, particularly because the Aggies should have been in the Cotton Bowl. Additionally, the Aggies broke with long tradition in 1994 by announcing that Texas A&M was leaving the Southwest Conference. On a bright note, the Aggie Band celebrated its 100th birthday in 1994, but students were shocked and saddened when a former band student became seriously ill while marching with other "Old Ags" during half-time ceremonies on Kyle Field. During the year Texas A&M got a new president, three new vice-presidents, its third new chancellor within a year, and a new chairwoman of the board of regents. It really had been a tough, turbulent, tumultuous year. Because of heavy rains, the 1994 bonfire began to shift as final logs were being carefully placed on the stack. But even that failed to dampen the Aggie spirit. Within a week, students and the community pulled together to dismantle and rebuild the bonfire—strong and sturdy. The Aggies went on to beat the University of Texas, so it really had not been a bad year—tough perhaps, but not a bad year.

And in some ways it had been a tough century—this past one hundred years—but by no means a bad century. After all, remember that the century began with the wolves literally encircling the little bastion

Courtesy Texas A&M University Photographic Services.

of higher public education that would one day become Texas A&M University. Through the years the wolves, at least symbolically, often seemed threatening. But the wolves only served to make A&M a little more determined and resolute.

The century ahead looked tremendously exciting and promising. There was a new, more dynamic Texas A&M University ready for a new century and a new, diverse, and strong community of colleges and universities now associated with Texas A&M "committed to assist students in their search for knowledge, to help them understand themselves and their cultural and physical environments, and to develop in them the wisdom and skills needed to assume responsibility in a democratic society." Texas A&M University had evolved and expanded "to meet the changing needs of state, national, and international communities."

That evolution had been particularly pronounced during the past quarter of a century. Times had often been tough. But that, Aggies thought, is really what life is all about. The real challenges that would confront Texas A&M University and the Aggies as they entered into the next century were not really from the outside world, from the wolves at the door; the real challenge was within, as had always been true. The challenge for students and faculty was to be all they can be. A university is more than legislation or buildings—it is people and ideas. A living, growing, changing, vital university is the complex mix of faculty, students, administrators, and former students who mold the character of a university and its graduates. It is the latter who are the measure of a university's success and greatness. Governor Richard Coke's admonition to those gathered for the dedicatory ceremonies of the state's first public institution of higher learning on that bald prairie on October 4, 1876, still holds: "Grave responsibilities rest upon you. The excellence of the college will be determined by your progress."